REACHING TO GOD - JOY

REACHING TO GOD - JOY

THE JOY OF HIS PRESENCE

R.A. MATHEWS

NAVI™ Publishing

EDITORS

"... in the abundance of counselors, there is victory."

— PROVERBS 11:14

Teresa Zintgraff Youhanaie
Alicia Byrd
Jane Charnock
Alice Powell
Janet Davis

The author obtained permission for the use of names and events in this book. Otherwise, all the characters, dialogue, and events herein are completely fictional, and any resemblance to actual persons, living or dead, or to actual dialogue or events is entirely coincidental and unintended. Fictional characters, dialogue, and events have been introduced in the spirit of Jesus' parables and should not be construed as real unless otherwise stated.

ABOUT THE AUTHOR

Acclaimed theologian Rev. R.A. Mathews graduated from the highest-ranked Baptist seminary in the nation with a Master of Divinity degree and four years of graduate study. She completed extensive Bible research thereafter from 2015 to 2024.

Mathews is an award-winning writer, and her weekly articles about the Lord have been published over 6,000 times in newspapers across the U.S. and overseas.

This volume contains both inspiring stories from the Bible and misunderstood Scripture—all supported with footnotes leading the reader to the verses in the Bible.

Mathews completed her university education at the age of 21 and started seminary that same year. She then sought ordination and was examined and approved by a panel of pastors and the association of American Baptist Churches to which her church belongs. She is perhaps the first Baptist woman to receive such an ordination in the South.

The Rev. Mathews subsequently worked in Christian broadcasting and in local churches, preaching and working with children and youth.

Like the Apostle Paul, she is bi-vocational, having graduated from a top ten ranked law school with an American Jurisprudence Award in mediation. She mediates disputes and represents children and the mentally challenged.

Mathews is the author of the *Reaching to God* series and a multi-volume serial novel, *Emerald Coast,* written under the pen name Red R.A. Mathews, which draws on her experiences as a state legislator.

She is the granddaughter of the Rev. Cora Hughes, an ordained Nazarene minister.

"I was reared in a family that dearly loved the Lord," she says, "and I gained a deep understanding of Him early on. I definitely had a head start on my spiritual path.

"The Lord is my all, as you will see.

"I hope these teachings about God comfort and strengthen your soul. But know that I am not perfect. Read the Scripture passages I have placed in the footnotes and please challenge me if you think I am mistaken. We take this voyage together."

ALSO BY R.A. MATHEWS

I. The Reaching to God Series

Available Now

Vol. 1 Reaching to God - Joy: The Joy of His Presence

Vol. 2 Reaching to God - Hope: The Hope of the Ages

Upcoming Release

Vol. 3 Reaching to God - Christmas: Oh Holy Night

Vol. 4 Reaching to God - Love: His Love Endures Forever

II. The Emerald Coast Series

Available Now

Vol. 1 Emerald Coast: The Vendetta

Upcoming Release

Vol. 2 Emerald Coast: The Fugitive

To my mom and dad,
who gave me everything.

Dedicated also to
Jay Thomas, Preston Boutwell, and David Ellis

ACKNOWLEDGMENTS

It is a pleasure to have many to thank for this book. I am grateful for the presence of each of you in my life.

I want to thank **Melanie Ezell**. You have such great insights, Mel, and showed me what I couldn't see! The Lord and I are grateful!

To my newspaper editors, **Josh Richards** and **Jay Thomas**: This book would not have flourished had you each not believed in me and kept publishing my thoughts. Thank you!

To **Preston Boutwell**, who made Bobby run and get a newspaper, and then shoved it at me, insisting I write something: Thank you. The Lord was in that moment!

I want to extend great love and appreciation to my editors: **Teresa Zintgraff Youhanaie, Alicia Byrd, Jane Charnock, Alice Powell,** and **Janet Davis.** You have my heartfelt thanks! You each gave generously of your time to proofread each word and then to send me notes. The book was truly a collaborative effort.

I must add, none of these bright, well-educated women should be blamed when I deviate from proper English grammar. Trust me, Ms. Alice made sure I knew better.

My thanks to **David Ellis**, who kept me from leaving my great little town, bringing me back to the house I adore.

A huge thank you to **Glen Collie** and the **Glasgow Cathedral** in Scotland for granting written permission for the use of the exquisite cover photo for the first and second editions. It was an honor!

I want to extend love and appreciation to my **Church Family.** Thank you for including me each week. I have come to love each of you individually. Your steadfast encouragement has meant more than I can say. Thank you!

A huge note of appreciation to the Patriarchs— **Mickey, Hoss, Bobby, Buddy, Danny, Pete, Lamar, Kenny, Preston,** and **John**—men of great faith, who lead by example. Thank you for including me. Iron sharpens iron.

I'm grateful to my "cover commentators," **Karin Patton, Melanie Ezell, Jackie Turley,** and **Teresa Youhanaie**. I appreciate you taking the time to look at what seemed like countless covers until we found the perfect one.

Finally, to my beta readers, **Rev. Pierce Mcintyre, Emily Mead,** and **Rebecca Brannon**: Your comments were always very helpful. Thank you for giving your time to this work!

CONTENTS

INTRODUCTION

Years ago, I heard a comedian making fun of his grandmother because she had a picture of Jesus hanging on her wall.

What's wrong with that? I thought, listening as the audience laughed. Apparently, not everyone loves pictures of the Lord.

I have many. My favorite is "Jesus laughing." I have two—one for home and one for my office. Also in my collection is a really old picture of Jesus kneeling in the Garden of Gethsemane. I could never part with it.

I also have quotes from the Bible displayed in the kitchen, bathroom, bedroom, study—wherever I spend time. My favorite: "'I know the plans I have for you,' declares the Lord, 'plans to prosper you and not to harm you, plans to give you hope and a future.'" Jer. 29:11 (NIV)

Honestly, I always want to be reminded of my faith. It is my greatest comfort.

I have never felt different from my friends. I grew up in a close-knit neighborhood. We all walked to school—that sort of environment. It never occurred to me to ask where my young friends went to church, or if they went to church. I think most did.

Looking back now, I imagine my home life was different from that of my friends. But you don't realize this as a child—you assume everyone lives the same way.

My mom's mom was an ordained minister, but both of my grandmothers were very devout. Their love for the Lord greatly influenced my parents, who passed their devotion along to my brother and me.

When I left for school each day, my mom made sure "A Mighty Fortress Is Our God" was playing, wafting around my brother and me, following us out the door. At the time, I hardly noticed, but now I see how deliberate it was. I can still hear that song playing in my memory.

At big family dinners, my cousins and I washed dishes as we sang hymns. I remember planning a family funeral with a new pastor, who didn't know my family. I suggested "In the Garden" for the grave-side service.

"Oh, no," he said. "We won't have hymnals."

I smiled. "Don't worry, we know all the verses."

When my aunt wanted to thank me for helping her, she bought me a new Bible. You don't want to know how many Bibles I own.

I was chosen over all my cousins and second cousins to inherit the cherished family heirloom. That precious piece is my grandmother's prayer table. Obviously, only one grandchild could have it, and my aunt (the Bible-giver above) passed it to me, deciding I was "the one."

I am the envy of my cousins over this, trust me.

Both of my grandmothers appear in stories in this book. In fact, many in my family will make their presence known. Most of these newspaper columns were written and published between 2015 and 2017. They reflect not just my walk with my heavenly Father, but the faith of those in my family who walked with Him long before I was born. It is the Presence of God through these many generations that radiates across the pages of this book.

I know growing up in such an environment gave me a head start, and I am grateful. But I am most thankful that the Lord trusted me to write for Him. Landing in my small town and penning the first article surprised me, as you will see. And He has remained my guiding hand.

I hope the truths in this book will bless you as much as they have blessed me.

PART I

STRENGTH FOR THE SOUL

"Unto thee, O God, do we give thanks . . ."

Psalm 75:1[1]

---

1. KJV

1

MARY AND ELIZABETH

TWO WOMEN WHO CELEBRATE BEFORE CHRISTMAS

". . . nothing is impossible with God."

LUKE 1:37[1]

---

1. NLT

TWO WOMEN WHO CELEBRATE
BEFORE CHRISTMAS

As a rule of thumb, you don't want to make an angel mad. But he did just that. And, honestly, it was so unlike this old priest. The Bible describes him as "righteous before God, walking blamelessly in all the commandments and statutes of the Lord."[1]

So what went wrong?

It seems the old man had his heart set on having a child before he died. He had prayed earnestly to God year after year. Then, suddenly, an angel appeared to him in the temple and said, "Do not be afraid, Zechariah, for your prayer has been heard."[2]

The angel said his old, barren wife would give birth to a son and to name him John. "And he will . . . make ready for the Lord a people prepared."[3]

That's when the trouble began—the holy man didn't believe the angel. And it gets worse. This was not your run-of-the-mill heavenly host.

"I am Gabriel," the angel announced. Can't you see him arching to

---

1. Luke 1:6, NASB
2. Luke 1:13, NASB
3. Luke 1:16-17, NASB

his full height, spreading his massive wings as far as they would go?[4] "I stand in the presence of God."[5]

Oooooh. See what I mean?

Listen closely and you can hear his words echoing off the gold and marble of the temple. This old priest needed to know with whom he was dealing.

And here it comes.

"Behold, you will be silent," Gabriel announced. "Unable to speak until the day these things take place, because you did not believe my words . . ."[6]

Gabriel left and six months later the angel was given one of the highest honors in heaven: Gabriel was sent with a message for a virgin. And what were her final words to him?

Mary said, "May it be done to me according to your word."[7]

Many think when Mary learned she would give birth by the Holy Spirit that she was afraid and kept quiet, only telling Joseph to whom she was engaged.

Not so. Look at the passage.

"Now at this time, Mary set out and went in a hurry to the hill country, to a city of Judah, and she entered the house of Zechariah and greeted Elizabeth."[8]

When Mary stepped inside the old woman's home, Scripture says the woman shouted, "Blessed are you among women, and blessed is the fruit of your womb!"[9]

This was Mary's cousin, Elizabeth. Obviously, the relative knew Mary was carrying the Messiah. Scripture says the old woman's words burst forth, coming from the Holy Spirit.

---

4. Full disclosure: Gabriel may or may not have had wings. Sometimes angels appear as ordinary men but at other times their appearance creates fear. This was one of the fearful times. It would seem that he did not look simply like a man, hence my reference to the wings.
5. Luke 1:19, ESV
6. Luke 1:20, ESV
7. Luke 1:38, ESV
8. Luke 1:39-40, NASB
9. Luke 1:42, NIV

Elizabeth said, "And why is this granted to me, that the mother of my Lord should come to me?"[10]

If you give that some thought, it's an amazing moment. This old woman and young virgin are similarly situated. How so?

One was too old to give birth yet six months pregnant. The other was a virgin but also with child.

The impossible made possible.

Mary stayed with her cousins, Elizabeth and, yes, old Zechariah, until their child arrived. Six months later, Jesus was born.

Many believe this was a fearful time for Mary. Not so. Look at the Biblical accounts of those months. Luke paints a vivid picture of Mary celebrating. He writes of her singing, "My soul exalts the Lord . . . the Mighty One has done great things for me . . ."[11]

And why not celebrate?

Both women now know the outcome of the prophecies, hundreds of years old:

"A voice cries, 'In the wilderness, prepare the way of the LORD; make straight in the desert a highway for our God.'" Isaiah 40:3[12]

"Behold, a virgin will be with child and bear a son, and she will call his name Immanuel." Isaiah 7:14[13]

Both Mary and Elizabeth now know the who of those prophecies, the when of those hoped-for promises, and the where—the very place Scripture would be fulfilled.

It's an exciting time!

Can't you see the two cooking and singing, dancing and praising God, chatting joyously? And then there is poor old Zechariah, who can't utter a peep—because he did not trust God.

Don't make that same mistake. Believe! When you earnestly pray, believe! Listen to the final words Gabriel speaks to Mary. Memorize them. "…nothing is impossible with God."[14]

---

10. Luke 1:43, NASB
11. Luke 1:46-49, NASB
12. ESV
13. NASB
14. Luke 1:37, NLT

Notes, Revelation, Prayers

Date:_____

If God moved in your heart, record your notes, revelation, prayers.

2

JEREMIAH

YOU NEVER FAIL UNTIL YOU GIVE UP

"'For I know the plans I have for you,' declares the Lord, 'plans to prosper you and not to harm you, plans to give you hope and a future.'"

JEREMIAH 29:11[1]

---

1. NIV

YOU NEVER FAIL UNTIL YOU GIVE UP

A hijacking occurred in the South recently. This sort of incident doesn't arise often. It took place in a little country town at the Methodist Church.

I happen to know that "Hijacking 101" isn't taught in seminary—a pastor is never going to be prepared. But this minister had four rowdy boys, and he rose to the occasion, bringing his life experience to bear on the situation.

The pastor gently stepped forward toward the outlaw, the hijacking still in progress. The boy kept on. The minister moved closer. The reverend then invited the boy to pray.

I was in the back and couldn't see as well as others at the scene, but I suspect everyone in that congregation wondered what would happen next.

Immediately, it became clear that the desperado had been reared in a God-fearing, Christian home. The tow-haired boy stopped. He responded to the request for prayer and bowed his head—all of his three-year-old self.

To be clear, the tyke had hijacked the children's sermon.

In the midst of the preacher's talk, the boy had suddenly effervesced with one comment after another, the pastor unable to get a word in edgewise. But the little guy surrendered when asked to pray. As I said, definitely reared in a devout home.

"Thank you," the boy began, "for food . . . and . . . the church . . . and . . . my toys . . . and . . ."

It went on and on.

He had lots of "ands"—a thankful child. When the little guy finally finished, he lifted his head and abruptly turned. The boy was not a novice; he knew how things went. Prayer signaled that childrens' time was over. The child raced down the aisle to his proud parents as they beamed with joy.

The whole church grinned.

I think the choir sang after that and there were some readings, but laughter erupted again when the pastor began the sermon. In addition to tiny-tyke hijackings, the minister said school hadn't prepared him for hospital visitations.

"Patients tend to undress," he said. "Apparently, it's important for God's man to see their scars."

So the sermon was about scars, and he segued into a different kind of scar. The ones you can't see. The emotional ones we carry through life. Our failures.

I leaned forward. Who can't relate to this?

It was a particularly good sermon and I'm a Baptist. Listen, we shout "Amen!" when the Spirit moves us.

But I'm not a babe in the woods with more reserved denominations. I learned my lesson long ago. I know whole congregations of Methodists and Presbyterians will turn and stare at such behavior.

I kept quiet.

As he preached, famous failures came to mind.

Engineer Soichiro Honda left Toyota unemployed, made a motorcycle, and eventually became a billionaire. Sidney Poitier was told at his first audition to "go be a dishwasher or something."

"Colonel" Sanders' chicken recipe was rejected by over a thousand restaurants. Vincent Van Gogh never sold a painting, except to a friend. Today, a Van Gogh can sell for over a hundred million dollars.

Dr. Seuss' first book was rejected by twenty-seven publishers. Dick

Cheney flunked out of Yale—twice. Jerry Seinfeld was booed off stage during his first try at stand-up.

Perhaps you remember how Fred Astaire was described after an audition? "Can't act. Can't sing. Slightly bald. Can dance a little."

Harrison Ford was told he couldn't make it, and modeling agents advised Marilyn Monroe to become a secretary. Lucille Ball was a B-list actress and encouraged to find another career. Charlie Chaplin was also rejected. His act was too "obscure." To say the least!

Steven Spielberg tried to get into USC's film school three times. He never got in. Stephen King tossed "Carrie" into a trashcan. It was his wife who helped him not give up.

And Monet was mocked for impressionism. I can't take my eyes off a Monet. Just amazing!

Elvis was fired from the Grand Ole Opry and told, "to go back to driving a truck." What if he had stopped singing?

Henry Ford failed five times until he finally succeeded with his Ford Motor Company. Harry Truman's business went bankrupt.

Think Macy's department store, think seven unsuccessful businesses beforehand.

Walt Disney was fired because he "lacked imagination." He also didn't let bankruptcy after bankruptcy stop him.

Einstein couldn't talk as a baby and was deemed mentally handicapped. Bill Gates dropped out of Harvard and his first company failed. Obviously, he didn't quit.

The Wright brothers were mocked for their flying machines, which they couldn't get off the ground. Winston Churchill not only flunked out of school as a child but was defeated at every run for office until he became Prime Minister at sixty-two. Failure didn't slow him down.

And who doesn't know the story of writer J.K. Rowling? She was an unemployed single mother on welfare when she wrote *Harry Potter*. But Rowling believed in herself and became a billionaire.

Thomas Edison made one thousand tries at the light bulb. What if he'd quit at the six-hundredth failure? Could anyone have blamed him?

During his career, Michael Jordan missed more than nine thousand baskets. He said all those failures were the reason he succeeded.

The minister that day at the Methodist Church skillfully aborted the hijacking of his service by asking the child to pray.

Prayer is also the answer to failure.

There's one particular area of my life where I am a complete failure. I try. I fail. I try again. I fail again. And I try yet again.

You can come to a point where you think it's hopeless.

After church, I talked the matter over with God, and I'm starting anew. Yes, prayer will change a heart.

The prophet Jeremiah, born mid-seventh century B.C., was thrilled when part of the Law was discovered in the temple—the main section of Deuteronomy. The children of God had wandered from their faith in the Lord, even engaging in the sacrifice of their children to win favor from gods.

Jeremiah thought Moses' Law would change their lives.

Subsequently, Jeremiah realized people don't change their ways until they have a change of heart. And he knew for a heart to change you need God.

There's comfort and hope in the words God gave Jeremiah. "'For I know the plans I have for you,' declares the Lord, 'plans to prosper you and not to harm you, plans to give you hope and a future.'"[1]

The pastor concluded his sermon that Sunday morning by assuring his congregation that God says, "Do it again! Do it again! Do it again!"

Remember, you never fail until you give up.

---

1. Jer. 29:11 NIV

Notes, Revelation, Prayers Date:_____
If God moved in your heart, record your notes, revelation, prayers.

3

BOAZ

ALL HE WANTED TO DO WAS HELP HER

"Give and it will be given to you."

LUKE 6:38[1]

---

1. NIV

HE JUST WANTED TO HELP HER

H e just wanted to help her. That's all it was. At first.
It was spring in Bethlehem and the fields of gold were ripe
for harvest. His men were already cutting the barley when he spotted
her working alongside his women, gathering the leftover crop.

"Whose young woman is this?"[1] he asked his foreman and learned
that Ruth was a widow from a neighboring country, now living in
Bethlehem for a noble reason.

"She has [worked] from early morning until now," the foreman
said, "except for a short rest."[2]

Immediately, Boaz left his foreman and went to Ruth—she needed
to know there was danger in other fields, men who would assault her.

"Keep close to my young women," he said. "And when you are
thirsty . . . drink [water] the young men have drawn."[3]

"Why?" She doesn't understand his kindness.[4]

Boaz told her that he had learned how her in-laws left Bethlehem
during a famine. The sons married and died. So did the father. The old

1. Ruth 2:5, ESV
2. Ruth 2:7, ESV
3. Ruth 2:8 ESV
4. Ruth 2:9, ESV

mother, alone now, wanted to return home, and Ruth had left everything to come with her mother-in-law.

Boaz was impressed.

At mealtime, he invited her to eat with them and quietly told his men to leave extra crop behind for her.

When Ruth went home that evening, laden with grain, she told Naomi, her mother-in-law, the day's events.

"The man is a close relative of ours," Naomi said, probably overjoyed. "One of our redeemers."[5]

A redeemer was a relative who could marry a childless widow, like Ruth, so an heir could be born to inherit the land.

Ruth continued working in his fields throughout the harvest, and then her mother-in-law devised a plan to ensure her daughter-in-law's security.

Ruth did as she was told—getting dressed, going to where Boaz and his men were threshing grain, and hiding until nightfall. Once Boaz fell asleep, she uncovered his feet and laid down. Boaz was then startled in the night and realized a woman was at his feet.

"Who are you?" he asked. It was pitch dark.[6]

"I am Ruth . . . spread your wings . . . for you are a redeemer."[7]

Whoa! She's asking him to marry her!

Honestly, when you read this book, you wonder if Naomi was a tad bit crazy. Why didn't they invite Boaz for dinner? Can you imagine any woman lying down beside her employer at midnight? Then asking him to marry her?

Even Naomi didn't know how this would end. She had told her daughter-in-law, "He will tell you what to do."[8]

Ruth knew Boaz had felt pity for her, but that didn't mean he would welcome a proposal on a threshing floor in the middle of the night. He could say, "Go home!"

I bet you want me to get on with it. What does Boaz do?

---

5. Luke 2:20 ESV
6. Luke 3:9, ESV
7. Luke 3:9, ESV
8. Luke 3:4, ESV

He accepts!

"May you be blessed by the Lord," he says. Then Boaz adds something more interesting. "You have made this last kindness greater than the first . . ."[9]

The first was leaving her family to return with her mother-in-law, but how is this proposal a kindness? A poor, young widow wanting a wealthy landowner?

Here it is, listen to what Boaz says. "You have not gone after young men . . ."[10]

Boaz felt bad about his age.

We all have such insecurities—things we can't change, things we feel another may reject. Some are obvious like age or size, but others are hidden—a disease, a debt, a conviction, impotence.

Boaz is thrilled.

He doesn't care about his work any longer, quickly leaving the threshing floor to fulfill the complicated requirements to marry Ruth.

"Ruth" is the eighth book of the Bible. Is it just a fanciful tale, or did these people actually live?

The writer plainly tells us the answer. Ruth's child is Obed, whose son is Jesse, whose son is David (as in slingshot David who fights Goliath). And David becomes king of Israel.

Ruth and Boaz were real people. They lived over 3,000 years ago, and you will see them again in Jesus' ancestry, which begins the New Testament.

Boaz helped Ruth and Naomi, expecting nothing in return, but they ended up helping him more. Although Boaz was a successful man, he was unsure of himself. Perhaps he had resigned himself to a life without marriage.

Jesus said, "Give and it will be given to you." [11]

No matter who you are, God will send people in need. The person you help today may help you tomorrow. This is God's way.

---

9. Luke 3:10, ESV
10. Luke 3:10, ESV
11. Luke 6:38, ESV

Notes, Revelation, Prayers Date:_____

If God moved in your heart, record your notes, revelation, prayers.

4

JOSEPH

READY FOR GOD TO SHOW YOU THE FUTURE?

"Trust in the Lord with all your heart and lean not on your own understanding, in all your ways acknowledge Him and He will make straight your paths."

PROVERBS 3:5-6[1]

---

1. NIV

READY FOR GOD TO SHOW YOU THE FUTURE?

Have you ever felt strangely drawn to act in some way and only afterward understood why—realizing God had shown you the future?

My grandfather owned a neighborhood grocery store several blocks from their family home. On a dark night, my grandmother suddenly grabbed one of his hats, sensing he was in danger. She shoved her hair beneath it, dressed as a man, and hurried to his store. Charging through the front door, she found a robber with my grandfather.

Immediately, the thief bolted and ran.

This grandmother, my mom's mom, was an ordained Nazarene minister, renowned for her faithfulness to God. The Lord showed her the future that night.

Many in the Bible were shown the future, but perhaps the most important was Joseph, Jesus' father. I'll show you why.

Preachers and academics alike will tell you that we know little about this Joseph. Not so—what the Bible tells us is profound. Joseph is the person in Scripture whom God trusted above all others. God's revelations to Joseph clearly show this.

Jesus may have lain in a lone manger surrounded by the gentle sounds of animals and later before doting Wise Men, but imminent evil threatened the Lord.

Newborn babies, infants crawling on hands and knees, and toddlers taking their first steps would soon be ripped from their mothers' arms and murdered. Jesus should have been among them, but an angel came to Joseph in a dream saying, "…flee into Egypt, and stay there until I tell you, for Herod will seek the young child to destroy him."[1]

It must have felt bizarre to Joseph—the virgin birth, the bright star hovering above, the wise men bringing unbelievable treasure.

Why leave such a celebration?

"Just a dream!" his family may have said. "Egypt is a long way. You don't know anyone there. Why go?"

Joseph knew exactly why—God had shown him the future.

The Bible doesn't have to tell us the strength of the relationship between God and Joseph. It's obvious. God had to be sure the father of our Lord would not hesitate, would not doubt the angel in the dream— even for a moment. The life of baby Jesus depended on it.

Joseph arose and fled in the night with Mary and baby Jesus.[2]

See the level of trust between the two?

That didn't happen overnight. Joseph had shown his loyalty to God for a lifetime, and God decided He could trust Joseph above all others.

That's big!

There were four dreams in all. First, that Mary would give birth via the Holy Spirit, which sounds common to us, but Joseph needed real conviction to believe that one. He also needed great faith to follow the angel's words in the second dream—to quickly flee. The final two dreams were to return and then settle in a safe area.[3]

Many in the Bible knew of impending events. Elijah knew of the coming drought, Daniel knew of the destruction of the temple, and Samuel knew Saul would lose his kingdom. Like Joseph, they were men chosen to do great things.

---

1. Matthew 2:13, World English Bible
2. Matthew 2:14
3. Matthew 1:20; 2:13, 19-20, 22

But God also calls in the smallest of things.

Take the man with the jug, living two thousand years ago.

One day, he felt strangely drawn to the edge of the city where he met two men. The two followed him home and then spoke with the head of the household, asking to see the guest room.

Only later would the man with the jug know the role he played for God. Jesus arrived that evening with the twelve and ate dinner in the upstairs room. It was the Last Supper.

The two men who followed the man with the jug were Peter and John. Jesus had told these two disciples that a man with a jar of water would be waiting for them at the edge of the city and would lead them to the house.

Jesus had also directed Peter and John to approach the master of the house, to ask to be shown the large, furnished upper room.[4]

Jesus knew all of this would happen.

The man with the jug had no idea. He only knew that he felt led to meet two men at the edge of the city.

Must you be special to be led by God?

The man with the jug isn't even named in the Bible.

Perhaps, as the years passed, the man with the jug forgot about his deed. I hope not—he was specially chosen to act for the Lord. God must have known when He placed the deed in this man's heart that the man would obey.

You too may be guided by a feeling, a vision, a dream, or a series of events too coincidental to be sheer coincidence.

You may even be led by a miracle.

As we get toward the end of this book, I'm going to show you how a miracle led me. My big-fish tale. There are witnesses, lest anyone doubt what happened.

That miracle changed the course of my life.

Draw close to God every day.

Pray to understand His way of speaking to you. As you learn to see Him leading and then act upon His guidance, trust will develop. It's the

---

4. Luke 22:7-13

kind of trust that Joseph, my grandmother, and the man with the jug shared with God. The kind that led all three to act without question.

"Trust in the Lord with all your heart and lean not on your own understanding. In all your ways acknowledge Him and He will make straight your paths."[5]

The more you trust and act upon God's leading, the more you will be shown.

---

5. Proverbs 3:5-6 NIV

Notes, Revelation, Prayers Date:_____
If God moved in your heart, record your notes, revelation, prayers.

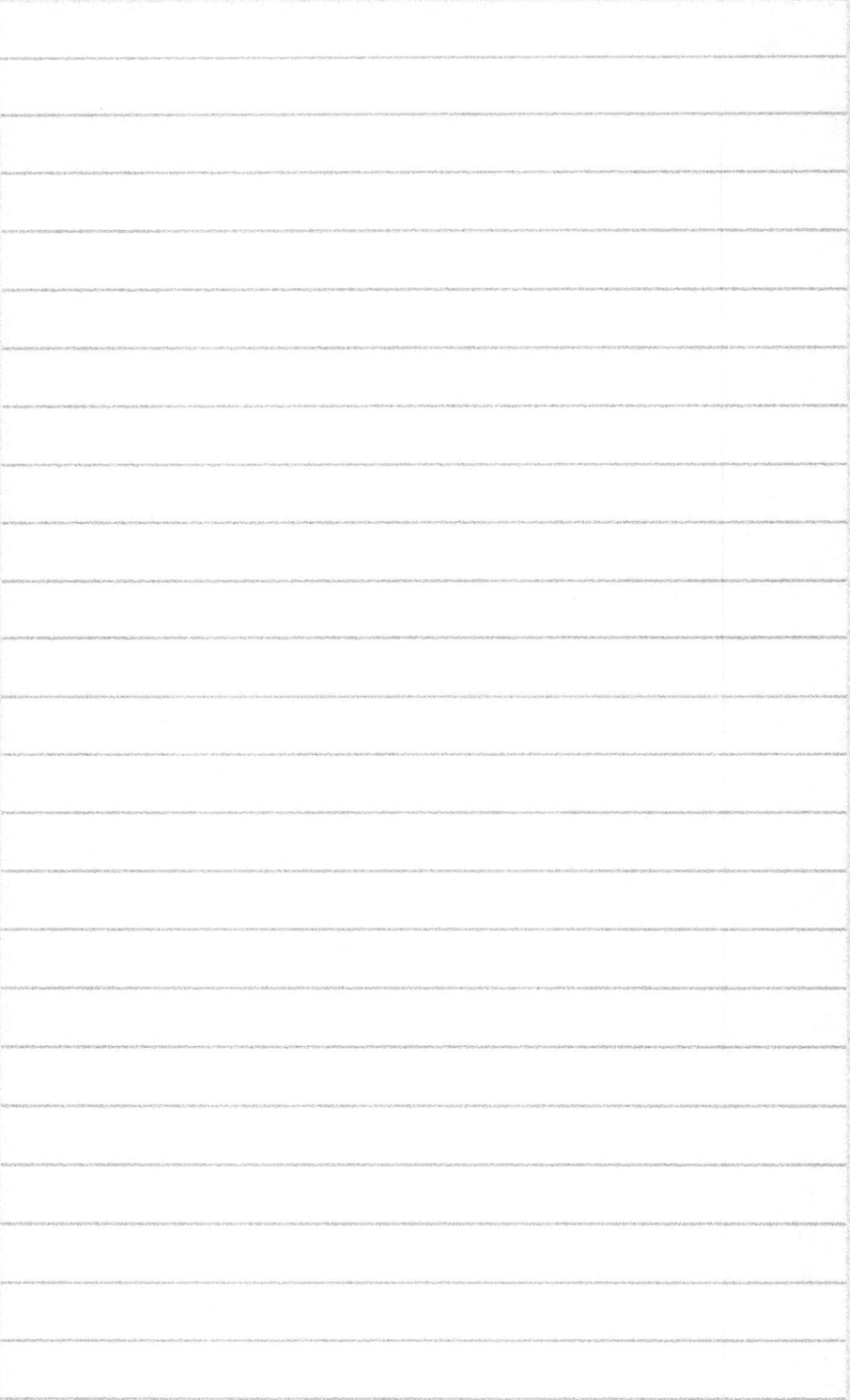

5

ISAIAH

THE BAREFOOT AND BARE BUTTOCKS
BILLBOARD

"You shall have no other gods before me."

EXODUS 20:3[1]

---

1. NASB

THE BAREFOOT AND BARE
BUTTOCKS BILLBOARD

I t's not "Daniel and the Lion's Den" nor "David and Goliath." It's a lesser-known Bible story—"Barefoot and Bare Buttocks."

I gasped the first time I read it.

A holy man walked naked and barefoot among the Israelites for three whole years. Immediately, I took a survey of friends, wondering who else knew.

No one.

"Was he crazy?" I was asked over and over again.

No. Nor is he an obscure fellow. I think both Jesus and the Apostle Paul quote him more than any other prophet.

When John the Baptist proclaims, "I am a voice of one crying in the wilderness, 'Make straight the way of the Lord,'"[1] he is quoting words that were written by this prophet 700 years earlier.

It's Isaiah.

Did I hear you gasp? Exactly!

I think of him as a grand person. Isaiah wrote: "For unto us a child

---

1.   John 1:23, NASB

is born, unto us a Son is given . . . and his name shall be called Wonderful . . ."[2]

Handel placed that amazing prophecy in his musical masterpiece, *The Messiah*.

Yet, in Chapter 20 of Isaiah, the prophet dropped his drawers (technically, it's sackcloth). The year is c. 711 B.C. Isaiah then went barefoot and naked for three years. Here's the passage.

"In the year that the commander came to Ashdod . . . the Lord spoke through Isaiah the son of Amoz, saying, 'Go and loosen the sackcloth from your hips and take your sandals off your feet.' And he did so, going naked and barefoot. Then the Lord said, 'Just as my servant Isaiah has gone stripped and barefoot for three years . . . so the king of Assyria will lead away stripped and barefoot the Egyptian captives . . . with buttocks bared . . .'"[3]

Can you imagine your children staring at the sight of a wandering naked preacher? For three years!

And why?

God had a point to make and Isaiah was chosen. The prophet became God's human ad—a TV commercial without the television. A billboard display without the billboard.

But naked?

The message was that important. God wanted to make sure no one forgot it. Every life would depend on their faith in Him. Here's what was going on.

In the eighth century BC, Assyrian King Tiglath-pileser III created a well-trained, well-armed military and conquered a sizable amount of the known world. He also invaded Israel. My kitten is named Tiglath-pileser IV due to a similar marauding nature.

After Tiglath's death, Northern Israel rebelled and stopped paying tribute to Assyria. Instead of the children of God turning to Him, they looked to Egypt for help.

The Lord and His commandments were cast aside as worthless.

---

2. Isaiah 9:6, KJV
3. Isaiah 20:1-5, NASB 1995

There was such wickedness in Northern Israel that the people even burned their children as offerings to gods, trying to win the favor of idols.

The Lord was furious—so angry that He destroyed Northern Israel, allowing the new king of Assyria to take His children into captivity.

Ten years later, God called Isaiah to walk naked. It was a warning for Judah (Southern Israel) not to trust Egypt. To trust Him. And to clean up their act.

Hezekiah, king of Judah, got the message and instituted massive reforms to win God's favor. The people did all that Hezekiah asked. No one wanted to be led away by an enemy, barefoot and naked.

The Assyrians had demanded tribute from Hezekiah and he had paid it, but he rebelled. That's when more than a hundred thousand mighty Assyrian soldiers arrived at the gates of Jerusalem, the capital of Judah.

An Assyrian officer stood outside the city, shouting, "Behold, you are trusting in Egypt, that broken reed . . ."[4]

He kept on shouting, trying to scare God's people, saying they were "doomed to eat their own dung and drink their own urine"[5] if they didn't surrender.

God's people were afraid. Terrified, in fact. Assyria had conquered everything in sight and was promising some leniency if they would come out.

Then they recalled that human billboard. Who could forget the prophet's bare buttocks? Isaiah probably wore a loincloth, but that's not clear. Scripture says he was naked.

This much is certain, God wanted them to stare. The Lord wanted His warning emblazoned on their memories. They had to *see* their future—they were doomed if they didn't have faith in Him.

Judah's King Hezekiah turned to Isaiah as the Assyrians stood at the city gates, and the prophet looked into the future. Listen to what Isaiah said:

---

4. Isaiah 36:6, ESV
5. 2 Kings 18:27, NASB

"[The Assyrian king] shall hear a rumor and return to his own land, and I will make him fall by the sword in his own land."[6]

Indeed, the Assyrian king believed there was a homeland insurrection and immediately abandoned his siege of Jerusalem. The king returned home, and he was later assassinated there.

But the Lord also sent an angel, who killed 185,000 Assyrian soldiers encamped outside Jerusalem.[7] God's people had changed their ways, and God granted them His favor.

I'm not facing the terror of Assyrian pillage (unless you count Tiglath-pileser IV), but I want God's favor more than anything. I know to stay right with Him. We all know.

Hopefully, you and I won't look out tomorrow and see a wandering naked prophet, but it could happen. As surely as Judah had to change, this nation also needs to turn back to holiness.

Shunning God brings defeat. Staying close to God leads to success.

---

6. 2 Kings 19:7, ESV
7. 2 Kings 19:35

Notes, Revelation, Prayers Date:_____

If God moved in your heart, record your notes, revelation, prayers.

6

JUDAH

PERHAPS YOUR LIFE IS BETTER THAN YOU THINK

"I always thank my God . . ."

1 CORINTHIANS 1:4[1]

---

1. World English Bible

PERHAPS YOUR LIFE IS BETTER THAN YOU THINK

Just this one thing, and then I'll be happy. Have you ever thought that?

Cindy's puppy, lean and long-legged, cleared fences like a deer. Luckily, Alpha was a good-natured dog. No one minded him cheerfully roaming the neighborhood.

At least, not at first.

Alpha's only vice was that he chewed on the newspaper.

"If I could just break him," Cindy said, "I'd be happy."

Every morning, she'd wave the torn newspaper, scolding him. Alpha was a smart dog and it finally registered—this rolled-up paper is important. So Alpha stopped chewing on them.

The first morning when Cindy stepped out to find the newspaper intact, she praised Alpha. "Good boy!" In fact, she followed up with treats. Cindy finally had the one thing she wanted.

The next morning, her newspaper was nicely intact, but Cindy frowned. Alpha stood over three more papers, wagging his tail.

She said, "I could hear his inner dialogue." *More treats?*

"No, no!" Cindy shook the extra newspapers, and the dog covered his head with his paws. Clearly, Alpha knew he'd disappointed her.

The next morning, Cindy sighed with relief. Only Alpha and one newspaper lay on the front porch. "Wheww!"

She turned to get him treats. "Good boy!"

That's when she glanced toward the sidewalk and her heart sank. Evenly spaced, in a neat row, lay 15 newspapers.

Cindy later said, "I didn't realize how good my life was."

Alpha now lives in the country with a nice old couple.

Just like Cindy, 10 brothers also thought one thing would bring them happiness—getting rid of their half-brother, Joe, who was seventeen at the time.

They hated him.

But I'm not sure whether it was Joe's fault. They all worked together in their father's business, and the old man had given Joe the job of bringing him reports as to what was going on.

Perhaps the boy was too diligent—what the brothers might have labeled "disloyal." That's because Joe took home bad reports about them.

Maybe the teen lacked even more judgment. He would relay his dreams to his family, suggesting that he would be a great success, and everyone would admire him one day.

Whether you call Joe's behavior a "straightforward manner" or "tattling and bragging," none of those incidents was the final straw.

The decisive blow against Joe came from their father.

Understand the dynamics of this blended family. Joe's mother was the only woman the father had ever loved. And she had died.

Apparently, each time the old man looked into Joe's eyes, he saw his beloved wife. Simply put, this father treasured Joe more than his other boys, which hurt the ten deeply.

And the day of reckoning finally came.

Joe arrived at work in a brand-new expensive coat, and his half-brothers snapped. They would never be happy until Joe was dead. Yes, the 10 formed a plot to kill him.

It's the fourth oldest, the brother they all listened to, who changed the boy's fate. The respected brother made the decision to relocate Joe to a faraway home. And, believe me, it was not nearly as nice as Alpha's.

You may recognize this as a famous Bible story. It's "Joseph's Coat of Many Colors," which happened nearly two thousand years before the birth of Christ.[1]

The brothers promptly sold Joseph to a caravan of traders headed toward Egypt. Then they dipped that precious coat in blood and took it to their father.

Problem solved.

Brat gone.

Now, everyone would live happily ever after—that was all they wanted.

As it turned out, the sons were wrong. Here's what happened.

"So they took Joseph's tunic, and slaughtered a male goat, and dipped the tunic in the blood; and they sent the multicolored tunic and brought it to their father and said, 'We found this; please examine it to see whether it is your son's tunic or not.'

"Then he examined it and said, 'It is my son's tunic. A vicious animal has devoured him; Joseph has surely been torn to pieces!'

"So Jacob tore his clothes, and put on a sackcloth undergarment over his waist, and mourned for his son many days. Then all his sons and all his daughters got up to comfort him, but he refused to be comforted. And he said, 'Surely I will go down to Sheol in mourning for my son.' So his father wept for him."[2]

The 10 brothers watched as their old father grieved. As the passage said, his daughters came, but nothing could relieve the elderly man's pain. "I'll die mourning my son."

What the brothers thought would bring them happiness didn't at all. Day after day, year after year, they watched their father cry, saw the old man's body bent with sorrow.

It hit the most respected son the hardest. Judah knew what he had done.

---

1. Genesis 37-44 covers the full story
2. Genesis 37:31-35, NASB

Years later, Judah offered to leave his wife and sons for slavery in Egypt, rather than bring more grief to his father.[3] It's from this honorable son that Jesus will descend, and you can see why.

Maybe what you think will bring you happiness isn't what you need at all. A Bible teacher asked, "What if you woke up tomorrow and all you had was what you'd thanked God for yesterday?"

Cherish what you have.

Perhaps your life is better than you think it is.

---

3. Genesis 44:3-33

Notes, Revelation, Prayers Date:_____

If God moved in your heart, record your notes, revelation, prayers.

7

MY MOM

MY MOM'S MAGIC CAN BE YOUR MAGIC

". . . David would take his harp and play it . . . and Saul would be refreshed and be well . . ."

1 SAMUEL 16:23[1]

---

1. NASB

MY MOM'S MAGIC CAN BE YOUR MAGIC

"This year," he said. "This coming year, you will be dead." The man wasn't a fortune teller—he was a doctor. An oncologist.

He sat by her hospital bed on Christmas Eve, the night before one of the holiest of Christian holidays. She had been in a car accident and routine tests had shown Stage-IV breast cancer.

Dr. Jubelirer had never seen her before. She had been brutalized by a tumor that had been misdiagnosed as arthritis, and he had quickly relieved her pain. My mom looked at him with such gratitude. She smiled.

"Do you understand?" he asked in earnest. I think perhaps he moved closer, but I can't remember exactly.

I sat in a chair at the foot of her bed.

"You don't know," I said, my voice filled with belligerence. "You don't."

My dad had died the year before, and my mom was all I had left. She was my whole world.

He focused on her, explaining her upcoming demise. I think he said he had a "moral obligation" to tell her. I only think that because we heard it so often.

She kept smiling at him, which bewildered the good doctor. But this part was clear to me—my mom was not interested in his predictions. No one told her what to think.

A second specialist appeared the next morning—Christmas Day. They were opening radiation oncology just for her. He told me to call hospice, to get her on the waiting list.

"She'll be dead by February," he said. He had a responsibility to tell us.

We saw more doctors for one reason or another. "You are going to die very soon," each said, making clear their obligation.

She didn't die in February.

Not in March, April, May, or June.

Month after month passed.

I watched as my mom's oncologist gave her the very best care, and I grew to both love and trust Dr. Jubelirer. Accordingly, I began to take that Christmas Eve prediction more seriously.

"Will it be like a time bomb?" I asked as the next Christmas approached. She seemed much better to me, but I didn't know anything about cancer. "You said a year," I continued. "Will she die without warning?"

He shook his head, saying she was no longer on a death timeline. She was getting better.

But no other doctor agreed with him. We saw a heart specialist when the oncologist detected a murmur.

"She should be dead," the cardiologist announced.

So did the next three and all of the general practitioners. As I said, so many moral obligations.

My guess is that most patients would have been at least discouraged, if not depressed. And my mom did almost die—more than once.

Yet her attitude never wavered. I never saw her feel sorry for herself. Nothing got the best of my mom. Not ever.

She had a great relationship with God, and they had an unspoken secret. She employed God's holy magic in times of distress.

Magic? From God?

What was that?

Honestly, I should have known long before I did.

At the brisk age of two, I was introduced to choir. There were probably seven or eight of us—remember, we were two-year-olds. We had little lemon-colored robes with big red bows at the neck.

"*You* were the choir," my mom said.

According to her, as long as I sang, everyone sang. And when I stopped, everyone stopped.

"You would see a lady's hat," my mom said, "and get distracted."

As my mom told the story, the choir director would quickly wave to me. As soon as I saw him, I was back, bringing along the two-year-olds.

For a decade, choir was my joy, but at twelve I wanted out. That's when I had a rude awakening—choir was not optional. No amount of pleading worked with my mom, not about choir. I had to go.

Like I said, I should have caught on.

As I write this, Christmas morning, I am listening to Handel's *Messiah* and thinking of the last time I was at that concert with her. It was a yearly event at the Municipal Auditorium in my hometown.

When I left for school, as I said earlier, "A Mighty Fortress Is Our God" was always playing.

Do you see a thread here?

Long before scientists proved that music could help stroke patients recover, or that music greatly improved motor skills in those with neurological damage, my mom instinctively knew it was potent.

She loved the Gaither specials with their Southern Gospel music, and that became a daily treat during her illness.

The week of Christmas, four years from that fateful Christmas Eve, my mom passed to the Lord.

She never said it, but holy music was her magic. She believed it would get you through when nothing else could. That it could brighten, embolden, and inflate you when something sharp would come your way and try to deflate the ball of life.

Music does just that.

Don't take my word, try it. For a paltry $2.19 when I wrote this in 2015, you could have *Handel's Messiah by the London Philharmonic Choir and Orchestra* as a digital download from Amazon.

The whole thing!

You can put it right on your phone! Listen to it as you work on your laptop. (It's 2024 now as I update this book and I just read this chapter for the first time in years. I am on my laptop and that $2.19 complete version of the *Messiah* is playing.)

50 Classic Hymns by various artists and *Come to the Quiet* by John Michael Talbot remain my staple albums.

I like Southern Gospel, but I find joy in a boatload of contemporary Christian music. I can't begin to tell you all the wonderful artists but here is a small preview.

Just about anything by Steven Curtis Chapman is amazing. *8 Greatest Hits* by Phillips, Craig, and Dean; *Welcome to the New* by Mercy Me; "Come Away" and "Rooftops" - Jesus Culture; "Just Say Jesus"- 7eventh Time Down; *Come to the Well*, *Thrive*, and *Until the Whole World Knows* - Casting Crowns; *Steady my Heart* - Kari Jobe; *Love Come to Life* - Big Daddy Weave; *I Need a Miracle* - Third Day; *All the People Said Amen* - Matt Maher; *Live Like That* - Sidewalk Prophets; *By Your Side* - Tenth Avenue North. There's also Hillsong. And Toby Mac is a great Christian rocker!

Remember, I wrote this list in 2015. Many new and wonderful artists have arrived since then. Don't miss "There Was Jesus," with Zach Williams and Dolly Parton. I could go on and on.

This year, let holy music lift you, heal you, brighten your life. It's nothing short of magic.

Notes, Revelation, Prayers

If God moved in your heart, record your notes, revelation, prayers.

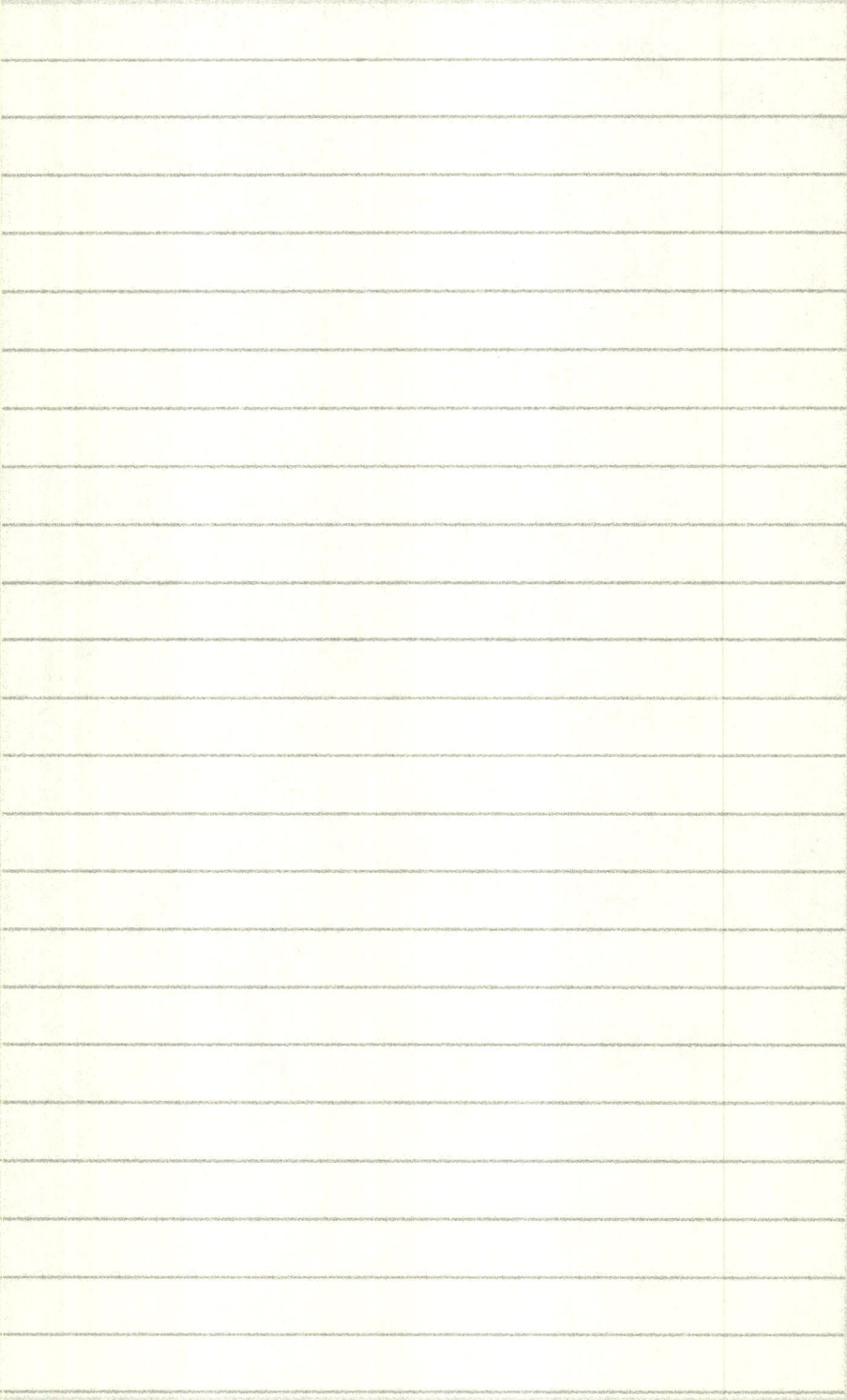

8

JEHU
THE SEXIEST MAN ALIVE!

"A good name is more desirable than great riches."

PROVERBS 22:1[1]

---

1. NIV

THE SEXIEST MAN ALIVE!

Had there been a "Hebrew People Magazine" or "Holy Land Enquirer," his picture would have rocked the cover as the "Sexiest Man Alive!"

The Bible says you knew he was coming long before you saw the warrior—he drove his chariot that furiously.

The man is Jehu, an army commander for Northern Israel.[1]

He could aim his bow and pierce the heart of an enemy without stopping. A man's man—definitely. But I suspect old women with wide, toothless grins stared as he passed.

Can't you see him strutting toward battle, tall and broad-shouldered, wearing his armor like a second skin? I certainly would have sought an introduction, smiling a little longer than necessary.

---

1. I often use "Northern Israel" and "Southern Israel" to make a passage less confusing, but that's not technically correct.

After King Solomon's reign, civil war split the nation in half. Scripture refers to Northern Israel simply as "Israel." You can see the potential for confusion.

Southern Israel is called "Judah," since the tribe of Judah made up much of Southern Israel.

I remember being chastised by a Teaching Assistant in seminary for not knowing the distinction. I hope to spare you my ignorance and pain.

Jehu's life is about to intersect with that of a young prophet. The two will change history. This is how the story played out.

It was roughly 800 years before the birth of Christ. Israel was at war with Syria and encamped at Ramoth-gilead along the border. Israel's commanders were in conference when the prophet appeared.

"I have a word for you, O commander," the prophet announced.

Prophets were revered. The word in Hebrew is "Navi," and when a Navi said, "Thus says the Lord," everyone stopped and listened. The Navi was about to speak the very words of God—what I call the red letters of the Old Testament.

Even so, I think those commanders looked over this guy and not in a good way. Before this encounter, the senior Navi had told the young prophet to tie up his robes before the prophet reached Jehu. So the man had come with his naked legs free beneath his robes.

I'm not making this up. He did that. I'll show you the Scripture in a minute and you'll see why.

So, the prophet arrived and said, "I have a word for you, O commander."

Jehu then asked which commander the prophet wanted.

"You, O commander."

Jehu and the ill-dressed prophet stepped inside the house. Minutes later, the prophet threw open the door and fled.

What do you bet Jehu's burly men guffawed—watching the man racing into the night in his mini skirt. Listen to what they said to their general: "Is all well? Why did this mad fellow come to you?"

Ah, the plot thickens—Jehu won't tell them!

He said, "You know the fellow and his talk."

But that was a Navi, and these soldiers, willing to fight to the death for Jehu, knew something was up.

"That is not true," they said. "Tell us now."

This is what was going on with the little guy. As I said, he had been sent by the biggest of prophets, the great Elisha, who had told him to tie up his robes and flee after completing the dangerous mission. Look at the exchange with Elisha.

"The prophet Elisha summoned a man from the company of the

prophets and said to him, 'Tuck your cloak into your belt, take this flask of olive oil with you and go to Ramoth Gilead. When you get there, look for Jehu son of Jehoshaphat, the son of Nimshi. Go to him, get him away from his companions and take him into an inner room. Then take the flask and pour the oil on his head and declare, "This is what the Lord says: I anoint you king over Israel." Then open the door and run; don't delay!'"[2]

Wow!

The little prophet was scared to death. What the man of God had done in that closed room was treason.

"'Thus says the Lord,'" Jehu then said to his men, repeating the prophet's words. "'I anoint you king over Israel.'"

Suddenly, there was an uproar! Every man stood and threw his garments on the steps before their commander.

"Jehu is king!" they proclaimed, blowing the trumpet.

But Jehu steadied them. "If this is your decision, then let no one slip out of the city . . ."

In other words, no one could warn the evil king.

Jehu mounted his chariot, and a company of men followed him.

Hours later, at the king's city, a watchman on the wall announced that men were coming. The watchman couldn't tell who they were, so the king sent out a horseman.

Jehu then shouted for the horseman to get in line behind him.

The watchman saw that. He relayed to the king what was happening, yet the watchman still couldn't see the man who was leading the company. But listen to what he said:

"The driving is like the driving of Jehu . . . for he drives furiously."[3]

I told you!

The king quickly raced his chariot past the strong walls to meet his general, undoubtedly thinking there was news from battle. Upon

---

2. 2 Kings 9:1-3, NIV
3. 2 Kings 9:20, NASB

reaching Jehu, the king suddenly realized treason was afoot, turned his royal chariot, and ran. Here's the passage:

"'Hitch up my chariot,' Joram ordered. And when it was hitched up, Joram king of Israel and Ahaziah king of Judah rode out, each in his own chariot, to meet Jehu. They met him at the plot of ground that had belonged to Naboth the Jezreelite. When Joram saw Jehu he asked, 'Have you come in peace, Jehu?'

"'How can there be peace,' Jehu replied, 'as long as all the idolatry and witchcraft of your mother Jezebel abound?'"

"Joram turned about and fled, calling out to Ahaziah, 'Treachery, Ahaziah!'"[4]

You know how this ends.

Jehu drew his bow with all his strength. The arrow sliced between the evil king's shoulders and pierced his heart.

Jehu, known as a man of strength and courage, lived up to his reputation that day. The Bible says, "Even a child is known by his deeds."[5]

One of the best parts of living in a small, Southern town is that people are "known." You live and die by your reputation.

What do you want to be known for?

Me? I want to be that nameless little guy with the naked white legs in the mini skirt. I want to be known as one who speaks for God.

And you?

Stop and consider this—what's most important to you? Live your life that way. Consciously make a choice every day for the reputation you want.

"A good name is more desirable than great riches."[6]

---

4. 2 Kings 9:21-23, NIV
5. Proverbs 20:11, NKJV
6. Proverbs 22:1, NIV

Notes, Revelation, Prayers

Date:_____

If God moved in your heart, record your notes, revelation, prayers.

9

BALAAM

WHEN BALAAM'S BAD ASS GOT THREE
WHOOPINGS!

"Choose this day whom you will serve . . . But as for me and my house, we will serve the Lord."

JOSHUA 24:15[1]

---

1. ESV

WHEN BALAAM'S BAD ASS GOT THREE WHOOPINGS!

This is the story of three ass whoopings.

Full disclosure: The ass in question is Balaam's donkey. And the animal was wrongfully whipped by its master, who happened to be a prophet. It's a memorable story in Scripture because the donkey then spoke to Balaam.

It should have also been a memorable moment for Balaam, but was it? We'll see.

I only knew of this one Balaam, whose story is in the Book of Numbers. Then, one day, I stumbled onto another Balaam passage while at my eye doctor's office.

I was alone, waiting in the exam room, when I suddenly shouted aloud. "No! Can't be. Not my Balaam!"

Thankfully, the door was closed because there I sat, Bible in hand, having a minor meltdown. I'd just read that Balaam, son of Beor, was killed by the Israelites.[1]

This Balaam, I thought, *son of Beor, has to be a different one.*

Dr. Carter entered in the midst of my crisis.

"I have to find something," I said, nose in my Bible. "Not the same

---
1. Joshua 13:22

one . . ." I babbled on. But there was too much to dissect, so I waited until I got home.

If you've never heard of Balaam, a first-century historian called him the greatest prophet of his time. I love those who speak for God, so I loved Balaam. Obviously.

But wait, had the Israelites killed *my* Balaam?

I had been reading in the Book of Joshua in Dr. Carter's office, the sixth book of the Bible, and I knew I was missing something. In my study at home, I flipped back to the story of Balaam in Numbers, the fourth book of the Bible.

Different books, I thought. *Not the same guy.*

God's people had left slavery in Egypt, wandered for 40 years, and then encamped beside the Promised Land in the country of Moab. They had defeated several mighty kings along the way, which made Moab's King Balak most uncomfortable.

Actually, he was scared witless, as you will see.

King Balak quickly sent for the prophet Balaam, determined to hire the famous man to destroy the Israelites.

But Balaam refused to return with the king's men, since God had directed Balaam not to curse the Israelites.[2] Balaam told King Balak's men that no amount of money could change his decision.

The king of Moab then sent princes with more money.

This time God said, ". . . go with them, but do only what I tell you."[3]

Here's where things get dicey and a bit confusing.

On the journey, Balaam's donkey took him into a field and then into a wall. The donkey finally sat down in the road.

Balaam beat the animal each time, and the donkey turned and spoke to his master.

"Am I in the habit of doing this to you?" the animal said.[4]

Only then did Balaam see the angel with the sword, ready to kill

2. Numbers 22:12
3. Numbers 22:20, NIV
4. Numbers 22:30, NIV

him. Immediately, Balaam spoke to the angel, ". . . if it's evil . . . I will turn back."

"Go with the men," the angel said, "but speak only the word that I tell you."[5]

What is going on?

First, Balaam won't go, and then God tells Balaam he can go. And now an angel is about to behead the prophet but changes his mind.

Honestly, I had never understood this passage, but I do now. Come along with me and I'll show you what happened.

So the prophet arrived in Moab and carefully spoke for God, refusing to curse the Israelites. But Moab's King Balak was not about to give up. Oh, no. He did everything but somersaults backward to get his way.

The king took Balaam and they sacrificed to God on seven altars. "Let's try over here," the king said again and again, desperate for a different result. They sacrificed in three different places.

Yet it's always the same. Balaam followed God's words and refused to curse the Israelites.[6]

So *my* Balaam was a good guy, right?

I had sat in my eye doctor's office saying that again and again. *This is my Balaam. A good guy. A prophet. A man of God.*

I had always loved Balaam.

Yet, the passage about the death of Balaam at the hand of the Israelites still worried me.

I read more carefully, searching the Bible for any mention of Balaam, trying to grasp the prophet's weakness, if he had one.

This is the passage immediately after Balaam returned home, seemingly having done nothing wrong.

" . . . the (Israelite men) began to commit infidelity with the daughters of Moab. For the (daughters of Moab) invited the (men of Israel) to the sacrifices of their gods, and the (men of Israel) ate and bowed

5. Numbers 22:35, NIV
6. Numbers 22-24

down to their gods. So Israel became followers of Baal of Peor, and the Lord was angry with Israel."[7]

The idolatry had brought a plague to Israel that had killed 24,000 people.[8]

It was no coincidence that this infidelity with the Moabite women and their gods happened right after Balaam left. The prophet had been behind it.

I found references in Scripture to Balaam being an opportunist.[9]

The prophet certainly had opportunity staring him in the face. The situation reminded me of a common saying among lawyers. "The best client is a rich one who's scared."

King Balak was just such a man. He was really afraid and willing to pay Balaam anything to get free of the Israelites. So, Balaam had to choose his path.

The day Balaam's ass (his donkey) got three whoopings was a day of reckoning for the prophet. The angel carrying the sword said, "I have come out to oppose you because your way is perverse . . ."

What does that mean?

Balaam should have had it uppermost in his mind. Remember, God had told Balaam he could go as long as Balaam stuck to God's message.

Therein lay the problem. Balaam had plans. If you look some 1,500 years later in the New Testament, Peter says Balaam "loved to earn money by doing wrong."[10]

So the angel was sent to set him straight. "I have come out to oppose you because your way is perverse . . ."

But Balaam didn't listen.

We clearly know that he did not curse the Israelites. But Balaam found a way to technically follow God and also satisfy the king. The Book of Numbers, as I said, doesn't tell what became of Balaam, and I

7. Numbers 25:1-3, NASB
8. Numbers 25:6-9
9. 2 Peter 2:15
10. 2 Peter 2:15, NLT

never knew. He died in the Book of Joshua, the passage I was reading in my eye doctor's office.

Balaam, yes my Balaam, was killed by the Israelites. Balaam didn't curse God's people, but the prophet showed King Balak how to do it.

The king didn't know about the Ten Commandments, didn't know that leading God's people to idols and adultery would turn God against the Israelites. Balaam educated him.[11]

And that's why the Israelites killed him.

It's the same today as it was then with Balaam: Leaders face choices. Some succeed while others fail, destroyed by their weakness.

Preachers succumb as well.

It's true for everyone. Your weakness is often what you don't have and want most. It should shout,"Danger! Danger! Warning! Warning!" Weakness is the place evil can easily enter if that weakness is not cautiously guarded.

God knows your heart as surely as He knew Balaam's. God will confront you just as He did the prophet. Listen to Him.

God can help you overcome anything if you acknowledge and surrender your weakness to Him. Examine your life and hand your weakness to the Lord while you still can.

Knowing where you are most likely to go wrong is the first step to change. Lay that at the feet of Jesus. Ask for help. Pray for guidance all day long.

Believe that God's grace is sufficient for you.[12]

---

11. Num. 31:14-17, Rev. 2:14, Jude 11
12. Unless otherwise stated, the Scripture quotations in this chapter are Numbers 22:20 (ESV), Numbers 22:34 (ESV), Numbers 22:32 (ESV), 2 Peter 2:15 (NLT), Numbers 22:35 (ESV), respectively.

Notes, Revelation, Prayers Date:_____

If God moved in your heart, record your notes, revelation, prayers.

10

THE CANAANITE WOMAN

POUNCE WITH ALL PAWS, WITHOUT PAUSE, AND HOLD ON

"I will not let you go unless you bless me."

GENESIS 32:26[1]

---

1. ESV

POUNCE WITH ALL PAWS, WITHOUT PAUSE, AND HOLD ON

S ometimes it's best to fight like a kid.

I started Sunday school when I was two. My grandmother, my dad's mom, was particular, so I was decked out in splendid array—embroidered little dress, white gloves, black patent leather shoes, my hair in curls.

Apparently, I didn't want to go.

First, as the story is told, there was the waving of the dress by my aunt like a bullfighter. "Come on!" she shouted, staring at me under the kitchen table, swinging the dress at her side.

I knew this was a trick.

"I want to look like David!" I shouted back. My brother, two years older, was in pants and a bow tie.

They finally got me dressed—I don't know the details, but I'm sure there was bribery involved. I know me.

So off to church we went.

My dad said he had to shove me through the door to the two-year-old class and quickly close it. The church had those two-way mirrors in Sunday school rooms, like the kind police stations use for line-ups. Parents could stand outside and watch their little ones without being seen.

"We waited," my dad said when he told me this story. "We weren't about to leave. You clung to the doorknob, crying."

As the story goes, a little boy approached me and slammed a plastic ball up the side of my head.

"And the war was on!" my dad said, laughing like it had happened yesterday. "You pounced on him with all paws." My dad wiped back tears of joy. "All you could see were the ruffled panties!"

Should we grapple with God like this?

Should we wrestle our Lord? Can we win?

You may be surprised at what the Bible says. Scripture gives many examples of those who followed Jesus, begging for help, but apparently, one woman was truly obnoxious. She wasn't merely shouting at our Lord, the Bible says she was *crying* at him, wanting healing for her child.

It must have gone on a long while and finally became intolerable for the disciples. They didn't gently ask Jesus to get rid of her, they *begged* him.

The Lord had said nothing throughout the ordeal. Then, when the disciples stopped and implored Him to act, she seized that moment. The woman quickly came and knelt at His feet.

I call her the "Heathen Woman"—she was not a child of God but belonged to people who worshipped evil gods. In fact, God had specifically, repeatedly, and adamantly told His people to have nothing to do with them.

Jesus made that clear when He spoke to her. "I was sent only to the lost sheep of the house of Israel . . . It is not good to take the children's bread and throw it to the dogs."[1]

Jesus called her a dog!

Listen, I don't think He did it with malice. Maybe He even said it with a smile, waiting for her response. I say that because Jesus did, in fact, go to the heathens.

For instance, when the Lord crossed the Sea of Galilee and healed

---

1. Matthew 15:24-26, ESV

Legion, that was not a Jewish region.[2] The same with the woman at the well. He was in Samaria, and Jesus reached out to many Samaritans through her.[3]

Another person might have walked away from Jesus that day, humiliated at being referred to as a dog. Many might have thrown the Lord an angry retort.

But the Heathen Woman was too desperate for any of that. She faced Him with no pride and is famous for saying, "Even the dogs eat the crumbs that fall from their master's table."[4]

And Jesus healed her child.[5]

Admittedly, she didn't actually wrestle God to the mat, but that woman was not going anywhere until she got what she wanted.

Jacob, on the other hand, did wrestle an angel of God and Jacob won. I am not kidding. It's in the Bible![6]

When good King Hezekiah was notified of his impending death by a prophet, the king begged the Lord to intervene. And God gave him fifteen more years.[7]

Even the downright evil can get their way—the despised King Ahab of Israel repented, and God granted him mercy.[8]

So, does this mean God changes?

God is the same yesterday, today, and tomorrow. He is all-knowing, all-powerful, forever in love with us. God does not change.

Nevertheless, God can choose to do anything He wants.

If He chose to bless a heathen woman and evil King Ahab, He can choose to bless you. God decides.

You can imagine my grandmother's face that Sunday morning. She probably offered me a course in behavior modification. It worked—proud to say I haven't decked anyone during this lifetime. But that

---

2. Mark 5
3. John 4
4. Matthew 15:27, NIV
5. Matthew 15:28
6. Genesis 32:22-30
7. 2 Kings 20:1-6
8. 1 Kings 21:20-29

childhood fight clearly demonstrates my God-given qualities: passion and determination. I'm grateful for each one.

When my dad was hospitalized and contracted a horrible infection in the hospital, he suffered terribly. I expected him to die and refused to leave, staying day and night. No one could love a father more than I loved mine.

In the evening, once he fell asleep, I would take the stairs to the chapel one floor above his room. Night after night, I knelt there and begged the Lord for another six months—I couldn't accept losing him.

That was in November. My dad recovered well enough to go home. May 31, six months later, he died at home.

The next year, as I said in Chapter 7, my mom developed a terminal illness, which doctors said would take her within months. She lived four years.

Usually, I pray leaving decisions to God, but I doggedly wrestled with Him for both of their lives. I needed them. And prayer moved His tender heart.

In times of desperate need, fiercely reach for God. Go at it like you did as a kid: Pounce with all paws, without pause, and hold on!

Notes, Revelation, Prayers Date:_____

If God moved in your heart, record your notes, revelation, prayers.

11

KING SOLOMON

THE DESTRUCTION OF THE GOLDEN AGE OF ISRAEL

"Above all else, guard your heart, for it is the wellspring of life."

PROVERBS 4:23[1]

_____

1. NIV

THE DESTRUCTION OF THE GOLDEN AGE OF ISRAEL

It was called the "Golden Age of Israel," beginning roughly a thousand years before Christ. This was the reign of Solomon, King David's son, which lasted forty years.

Scripture says, "King Solomon was greater in riches and wisdom than all the other kings of the earth."[1] The weight of the gold he received yearly was twenty-five tons. Every world ruler sought to speak with him, to hear the wisdom of God.

Pretty impressive.

Yet Solomon's story is one of the great tragedies of the Bible—he destroyed his kingdom by making one mistake.

Completely avoidable.

Perhaps Solomon knew what he had done wrong when he wrote this Proverb, "Above all else, guard your heart for it is the wellspring of life."[2]

I knew a devout woman who used to scratch her head over that verse. "What does it mean?" she would say. "Jesus wants us to keep our hearts open."

---

1. 1 Kings 10:23-27, NIV
2. Proverbs 4:23, NIV

This woman did not understand the verse, but you will. You're about to see why Solomon thought this way. To him, it was the most important thing: "Above all else . . ."

Here's why.

As soon as Solomon secured his throne, his first act was to make a treaty with Pharaoh, king of Egypt, and marry Pharaoh's daughter. Solomon loved many more foreign women, tallying up 700 wives and 300 concubines.

Yet God had carefully warned the Israelites about the women of Moab, Ammon, Edom, Sidon, and other foreign nations. He had said, "You must not intermarry with them because they will surely turn away your hearts after their gods."[3]

King Solomon thought he was too wise to let that happen.

But once Solomon grew old, his wives turned his heart toward their gods. And Solomon not only built altars for these idols, he also sacrificed to them.

It was unthinkable!

I still cannot believe it happened.

Solomon violated the First Commandment, no other gods. This was something his father never could have done.

God then said because of Solomon's evil, Israel would be torn apart.[4]

If you read the story of Balaam's ass in Chapter 9, you'll remember how Moab's King Balak did everything possible to get God to curse the Israelites during the Exodus. King Balak's story takes place roughly 500 years before Solomon's reign. The odd thing about King Balak is this: Why didn't Balak turn from his god and worship God, since Balak really believed God was all-powerful?

Moabites did convert and choose God.

Remember the famous woman in Chapter 3, who left Moab and that nation's god? Moabites worshiped Chemosh, yet Ruth accepted the one true God.

---

3. 1 Kings 11:2, NIV
4. 1 Kings 11:6-11

Ruth's great-grandson was King David. And, ironically, it's her great-great-grandson, Solomon, who introduced Chemosh worship to the Israelites.[5]

God was furious!

So, when Solomon wrote: "Above all else, guard your heart . . . ," perhaps he knew his mistake. Your heart can overrule your mind and your will.

The person you marry will bring you closer to God or tear you away from Him. Scripture says, "Do not be unequally yoked with unbelievers."[6]

After making a serious mistake in her dating life in college, a friend vowed that she wouldn't go out with a man unless she asked where he went to church.

"That was also a mistake," she said.

Why? Because, oh yes, they always said they went to church, could name their congregation right off, leaving out the part that they hadn't been there in ages. The better question: What was the sermon about last Sunday?

A person who doesn't go to church will begin backtracking immediately. It goes something like this: "I like church, but I'm usually stuck at work."

Or some other poor explanation.

Learn from my friend's mistake. Never be ashamed to want someone who loves the Lord. The man who laughs at that sermon question isn't the person for you.

The one who responds with a sincere answer will know why you're asking and respect you for it. Your goal isn't to impress anyone but God.

Even if you're happily married, this message is still for you. Your children and your grandchildren need guidance. More today than ever. Don't think they don't listen. Talk to them.

Simply put, in matters of the heart be very careful—love can bring

---

5. 1 Kings 11:7
6. 2 Corinthians 6:14 ESV

happiness or ruin. The sad truth is that the woman who couldn't understand Solomon's words, the woman I mentioned at the beginning of
this chapter, had married very badly. She paid for that one mistake her
whole life and so did her children.

As Solomon said: "Above all else, guard your heart, for it is the
wellspring of life."[7]

---

7. Proverbs 4:23, NIV

Notes, Revelation, Prayers

Date:_____

If God moved in your heart, record your notes, revelation, prayers.

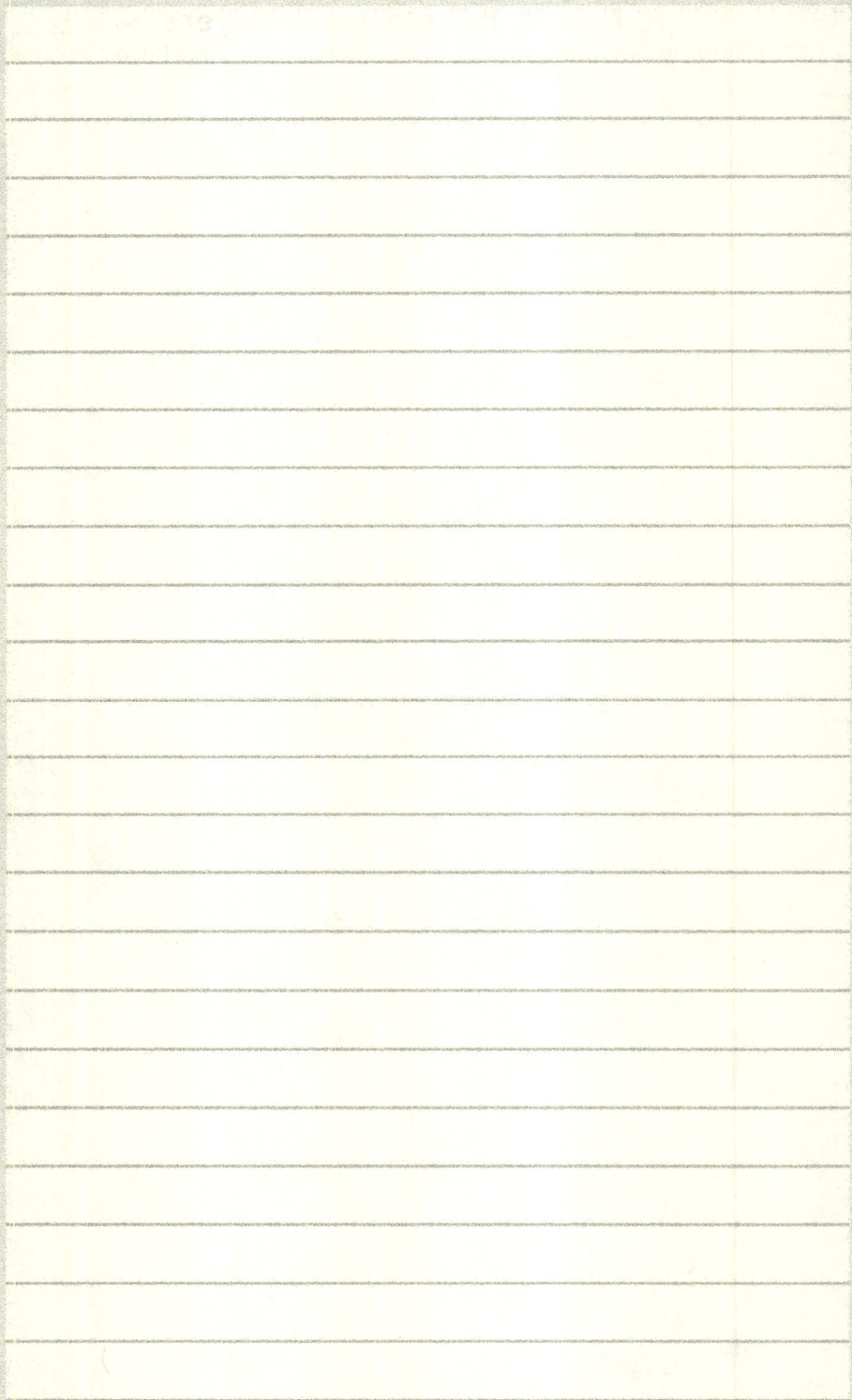

12

MY FRIEND

HOPE LOST AND FOUND

"Do not merely look out for your own personal interests, but also for the interests of others."

PHILEMON 2:4[1]

HOPE LOST AND FOUND

They tooled around in a '57 Chevy, both women approaching eighty, calling one another by their last names: "Smith" and "Wesson."[1]

Smith rode shotgun, she had never learned to drive, while Wesson clutched the wheel in a two-fisted, white-knuckled, we're-good-to-go grip. Wesson's coke-bottle glasses announced she was blind, but no one dared challenge the fierce duo.

It was inevitable that their granddaughters would become independent-minded lawyers. Age-wise, the girls were in five-year stair steps: Take-charge Whitney Wesson, Kind-hearted Suzie Smith, and Memorable Willa Wesson.

Willa always stood out—pretty and funny and blonde

After their grandmothers died, Whitney Wesson moved into her grandmother's house and Suzie Smith into Shotgun's house—just three blocks apart. In fact, Wesson's house sits on Smith Avenue, named for Shotgun-Smith's husband. Purely by coincidence.

I am not making this up.

I have changed the names and physical descriptions of people and

---

1. I changed their names to protect their privacy.

places to allow everyone privacy, but otherwise, this story is true. As I said, Wesson lived on a street named for Smith's husband, who was a city councilman. Again, the houses are three blocks apart.

On many nights, Suzie Smith would find herself sprawled across Whitney Wesson's hardwood floors. Suzie's pen would fire across the page as the more experienced Whitney explained a legal procedure.

Since lawyering is complex, most attorneys choose specialties. Kind-hearted Suzie gravitated toward clients she called *the patients*.

The patients never dressed up to see her—no lipstick or high heels. Most awakened not realizing their lives were about to change, that someone would be taking them to the courthouse.

They weren't criminals.

No. In fact, most seemed helpless. The patients had addictions or mental disabilities that had become life-threatening. Many states have laws that require hospitalization in these instances. But first, there must be a hearing.

Once the patients were secured at the courthouse, the U.S. Constitution requires that these people be represented by counsel. Suzie would step inside their little holding rooms, introduce herself, and explain the matter, saying she was there for them.

They came for various reasons, but many were suicidal.

Suzie had a counseling background and liked this work. She said people who lose hope kill themselves.

One day, Suzie represented a young mother, clearly exhausted by life. The mother had left her toddler with a cousin while she worked. The child had fought it, kicking and screaming. Only later did the mother learn why—there had been sexual abuse.

"He's better without me," the mother said about her child, weeping bitterly, hating herself.

Suzie then spoke separately with the woman's parents and sisters. They'd brought the child, who was now quite a bit older—his sad eyes said he knew what was going on.

Suzie took the adults aside, refusing to talk in front of the boy, and then Suzie went back to the mother. All Suzie could think was how everyone was continuing to hurt that child.

"He needs you," Suzie said.

The mother shook her head.

"Do you know what happens to children when a parent commits suicide?" Suzie asked.

The mother didn't lift her head.

"Statistically," Suzie continued, "they are more likely to take their lives."

The woman abruptly straightened and stared at Suzie—a mother's love kicking in.

Suzie told Whitney about that case. "As soon as she heard the statistic, the mother turned her life around."

Suzie had represented hundreds of suicidal patients, helping them realize they had good reason to soldier on.

"How's Willa doing out there?" Suzie asked.

Willa had reluctantly followed her husband's career to a faraway state. Suzie remembered how proud sweet Willa had been of her.

"She praised one of my accomplishments," Suzie said with a smile, "the last time I saw her."

"Getting divorced," Whitney said. "She's only staying there for her daughter."

Neither knew as they talked that Willa lay dead. Hours earlier, Willa had taken her life.

Suzie sat through the funeral thinking of their indomitable grandmothers, wondering what could have made a difference.

Willa had always carried a photo of her daughter.

Suzie knew if Willa had realized the impact the suicide would have on her child, Willa wouldn't have taken her life. If Willa had written on that photo, "My daughter will do what I do," it might have changed everything.

Both Suzie and Whitney wished Willa would have returned home.

If you're thinking of taking your life, go and be with someone you love. Really consider the impact it will have on your children, your parents, your siblings, and your grandparents.

Call or text the suicide hotline:

1-800-273-TALK
or
Text 741741.

They're available 24/7, and the call is confidential.

What to expect when texting a suicide hotline:

If you have never contacted a suicide hotline, here's exactly what happens. I sent a text to 741741 so you could see.

1:53 p.m. - My text: "Is this the text hotline?"

1:53 p.m. - Response: "Thanks for texting Crisis Text Line, where you'll text with a compassionate Crisis Counselor . . . what's on your mind?"

1:54 p.m. - My text: "Just wanted to see if the number worked."

1:54 p.m. - Response: "We're getting a crisis counselor for you. It may take a moment."

1:56 p.m. - Response: "Thanks for texting . . . we're 100% real! A group of trained counselors." (She then responded to my questions.)

What to expect when calling a suicide hotline:

If you have never called a suicide hotline, I did it today so I could tell you how it goes. **1- 800-273-TALK**

A friendly young woman answered within a minute.

She said, "What's going on?" She was ready to help with whatever the problem was.

I explained that I was writing about suicide and asked whether worried friends and family could also contact them.

"Definitely!" she said.

A friend of mine recently told me she was very depressed. She has financial problems from medical bills and a poor living situation. I told her to call me day, night, or in the middle of the night if she ever feels hopeless. I made her promise, but I will keep checking on her.

If you suspect a person has lost hope, intervene. Friends and family can call or text these numbers. Do that now. Get help today.

1-800-273-TALK

or

Text 741741.

We each need to pay attention. Scripture says: "Do not merely look out for your own personal interests, but also for the interests of others."[2]

You never know what another person is going through.

---

2. Philippians 2:4, NASB

Notes, Revelation, Prayers Date:_____

If God moved in your heart, record your notes, revelation, prayers.

13

BILLY GRAHAM

TAKE IT TO THE LORD IN PRAYER

". . . do not be anxious about anything, but in everything by prayer and supplication, with thanksgiving, let your requests be made known to God. And the peace of God, which surpasses all understanding, will guard your hearts and your minds in Christ Jesus."

PHILIPPIANS 4:6[1]

---

1. ESV

TAKE IT TO THE LORD IN PRAYER

I 've seen her several times in a store where I shop. She's hard to miss, always smiling, always a kind word for the workers there.

I noticed her the other day as she stopped before entering the place, saw her eyeing a man in the parking lot. Suddenly, it seemed as though a gale of sorrow swept over her.

She kept moving forward, her head down now, but clearly she'd been reminded of something unpleasant. One of the store's workers approached her as she stepped inside.

"Are you okay?" he asked.

I watched as she lifted her head and forced a smile. "Yes. Why?"

He hesitated, studying her. "You look so unhappy."

She shook her head. "It's nothing prayer can't fix."

I smiled. Her words reminded me of Billy Graham's favorite hymn. Here's how it goes:

What a friend we have in Jesus, all our sins and griefs to bear! What a privilege to carry everything to God in prayer!

O, what peace we often forfeit, O, what needless pain we bear, all because we do not carry everything to God in prayer.[1]

---

1. Written by Joseph Scriven (1820-1886).

Powerful words!

That same day, I overheard two people talking, a woman trying to help a man who seemed as though he was sinking.

"I believe," she said, "that God is the answer to all problems."

It's true. God will show you the right path and strengthen you on your way. He will comfort you in time of trouble. If you need a miracle, He is the God of miracles.

Listen to what happens when Paul and his disciple visit the early Christian churches. They're beaten in the marketplace and then thrown into jail.

At midnight, the other prisoners suddenly hear the two praying and singing hymns. Immediately, there's an earthquake—the prison doors are thrown open and all shackles are broken. The jailer, certain they've escaped and knowing it means death for him, draws his sword to take his life.

"Don't harm yourself!" Paul shouts. "We are all here!"

Paul will lead the jailer and his family to Jesus that night. The jailer will care for the two in his home, binding their wounds, and then return them to the prison.

At daylight, the magistrates send word to release Paul and his disciple, but Paul won't go. Paul is indignant, claiming the judges have unjustly imprisoned and beaten them.

When the magistrates hear this and discover that Paul is a Roman citizen, they fearfully come to the jail and apologize.[2]

Look at our God in action: What seemed a desperate situation turned into salvation for the jailer and victory for God!

I saw that prayerful woman from the store this past weekend, and she shared some of her life with me. She has known hardship, as Paul had in prison. We all have. Everyone needs help.

She went on to tell me about her devotional life. "Sometimes when I am discouraged," she said, "God reaches out and shows me a person in a wheelchair or with cancer. Seeing their terrible misfortune changes

2. Acts 16:16-40

everything. Immediately, it blots out any unhappiness inside me. I lift my heart and give thanks for all that God has given to me."

I nodded, knowing that feeling.

"At other times," she continued, "it takes a while to pray through my pain. God always sends an answer—maybe from another person, or sometimes I simply feel His guidance. Music really helps me."

"What kind of music?"

"Hymns."

I grinned, thinking of Paul singing hymns in prison,[3] and how Jesus and the disciples sang a hymn after the Last Supper.[4]

"Which ones do you like?" I asked.

She thought a moment. "I love 'Be Still My Soul,' but my favorite is 'What a Friend We Have in Jesus.'"

If you have forgotten all the words to that hymn, go online to YouTube. You'll be surprised to see how many mega stars have recorded "What a Friend We Have in Jesus." Like Billy Graham, they proudly sing of what they do when life gets rough:

They take it to the Lord in prayer.

The Scripture Passage
Acts 16:16-40
I included the full story from Acts. Trust me, it's a great read. This is Luke telling what happened.

"It happened that as we were going to the place of prayer, a slave woman who had a spirit of divination met us, who was bringing great profit to her masters by fortune-telling. She followed Paul and us and cried out repeatedly, saying, 'These men are bond-servants of the Most High God, who are proclaiming to you a way of salvation.' Now she continued doing this for many days. But Paul was greatly annoyed, and he turned and said to the spirit, 'I command you in the name of Jesus Christ to come out of her!' And it came out at that very moment.

3. Acts 16:25
4. Matthew 26:30

"But when her masters saw that their hope of profit was suddenly gone, they seized Paul and Silas and dragged them into the market-place before the authorities, and when they had brought them to the chief magistrates, they said, 'These men, Jews as they are, are causing our city trouble, and they are proclaiming customs that are not lawful for us to accept or to practice, since we are Romans.'

Paul and Silas Imprisoned

"The crowd joined in an attack against them, and the chief magistrates tore their robes off them and proceeded to order them to be beaten with rods. When they had struck them with many blows, they threw them into prison, commanding the jailer to guard them securely; and he, having received such a command, threw them into the inner prison and fastened their feet in the stocks.

"Now about midnight Paul and Silas were praying and singing hymns of praise to God, and the prisoners were listening to them; and suddenly there was a great earthquake, so that the foundations of the prison were shaken; and immediately all the doors were opened, and everyone's chains were unfastened. When the jailer awoke and saw the prison doors opened, he drew his sword and was about to kill himself, thinking that the prisoners had escaped. But Paul called out with a loud voice, saying, 'Do not harm yourself, for we are all here!' And the jailer asked for lights and rushed in, and trembling with fear, he fell down before Paul and Silas; and after he brought them out, he said, 'Sirs, what must I do to be saved?'

The Jailer Converted

"They said, 'Believe in the Lord Jesus, and you will be saved, you and your household.' And they spoke the word of God to him together with all who were in his house. And he took them that very hour of the night and washed their wounds, and immediately he was baptized, he and all his household. And he brought them into his house and set food before them, and was overjoyed, since he had become a believer in God together with his whole household.

The Magistrates Confronted

"Now when day came, the chief magistrates sent their officers, saying, 'Release those men.' And the jailer reported these words to Paul, saying, 'The chief magistrates have sent word that you be released. So come out now and go in peace.' But Paul said to them, 'After beating us in public without due process—men who are Romans —they threw us into prison; and now they are releasing us secretly? No indeed! On the contrary, let them come in person and lead us out.' The officers reported these words to the chief magistrates. And they became fearful when they heard that they were Romans, and they came and pleaded with them, and when they had led them out, they repeatedly asked them to leave the city. They left the prison and entered the house of Lydia, and when they saw the brothers and sisters, they encouraged them and departed."[5]

————

REMEMBER Paul's night in prayer and do the same. Take what you are facing to God.

---

5. Acts 16:16-40, NASB

Notes, Revelation, Prayers Date:_____

If God moved in your heart, record your notes, revelation, prayers.

14

TAMAR

"YEP, THAT WAS ONE BIG WHOOPSIE DOODLES!"

". . . Judah begat Perez and Zerah, whose mother was Tamar . . ."

Matthew 1:3[1]

---

1. NIV & KJV

"YEP, THAT WAS ONE BIG WHOOPSIE DOODLES!"

Whoopsie doodles—urban slang for a big mistake.

Early one morning, my friend Jane painstakingly made a beautiful cheese soufflé. She had just sat down to eat when Penny, her coonhound, hastened to the table.

"You're not getting any," Jane said. The big red dog stared at the soufflé. "Go away," my friend continued.

Penny immediately eyed a bag of cookies on the table, grabbed it, raced across the kitchen, out the dog door, and up a steep hill behind the house.

Now, my very bright dog would have promptly ripped that bag open and downed every one of those cookies. But Penny was different. Penny deserved a place in Mensa.

Once Jane scaled the hillside, Penny politely handed over the bag of baked goods.

"Nice dog!" Jane said.

Penny grinned, galloped down the hill, shoved through the dog door, and then raced into the house.

Jane said she stood on the hill, staring at the swinging dog door, mouth hanging open, knowing she had just been had by a coonhound.

Sure enough, Penny trotted through the kitchen, seated herself at the dining room table, and devoured one beautiful cheese soufflé.

That's a true whoopsie doodles.

Tamar is one of the best whoopsie doodles in the Bible. This story is a little bit steamy. Okay, it's a lot steamy—so cover your kids' eyes.

Tamar is mentioned in what I call "The Begats," which open the New Testament—Abraham begat Isaac, Isaac begat Jacob, Jacob begat Judah and so on. It's the ancestry.com for our Lord, tracking a span of 2,000 years from Abraham to Joseph and then Jesus.

Boring stuff, right? Hardly—just you wait and see!

Judah, fourth generation in the genealogy, marries and has three sons. His eldest son weds Tamar and then dies without an heir.

It was the duty of a brother-in-law to keep his brother's line alive, so Judah's second son marries Tamar. He also dies, also without a child.

Judah then tells Tamar to go to her father's house in another town and to live as a widow. He promises to let her wed his youngest son when the boy is of age.

Tamar agrees.

Years later, when the boy grows up, Judah's true intention becomes clear. He thinks the woman is a curse and isn't about to lose his last son to her.

Tamar realizes the promise will never be met. She knows that leaves her without an heir.

More time passes and Judah's wife dies. Here's the steamy part. Kids' eyes covered, right?

Judah is struck with grief but eventually returns to work. Tamar hears he will be passing by her town and devises a bold plan. She quickly sheds her widow's clothes, wears a veil to disguise herself, and poses as a prostitute, sitting on the road by the town.

Judah sees this woman in her veils and comes over to her. I'll let the Bible continue the story:

"Come, now, let me sleep with you," he says.

"What will you give me to sleep with you?" she asks.

"I'll send a goat from my flock."

"Will you give me something as a pledge until you send it?"[1]

Judah leaves his carved staff and several other items, all distinctive to him. He then returns home and sends the goat. But the woman can't be found.

"We have no town prostitute," the people there tell him.

Months later, Judah is informed that Tamar has played the harlot and is pregnant. He's furious.

"Bring her out and burn her!" he shouts.

She immediately sends a message to her father-in-law, along with the things she had taken as a pledge.

"I'm pregnant by the man who owns these," she says.

Of course he recognizes them. Judah also knows he's cheated her out of his third son and the possibility of an heir.

"She's in the right," he says. "I'm in the wrong."

Tamar bears twins and her first child will become the great, great, great, (add many more greats) grandfather of Jesus. See how Tamar ends up in The Begats.

Old Testament prophecy says the Messiah will descend from the tribe of Judah, but without Tamar that would not have happened.

The next time you read through Jesus' ancestry, hopefully you will think of the lives of those men and a few remarkable women. They were real people. Some had truly interesting and important stories— one quite saucy. In fact, when you see Judah and Tamar listed there, you may recall their lives and say:

"Yep, that was one big whoopsie doodles!"

---

1. Genesis 38:16-17, NIV

Notes, Revelation, Prayers

If God moved in your heart, record your notes, revelation, prayers.

15

TIGLATH-PILESER IV

FIVE WORDS

"The Lord is close to the brokenhearted . . ."

PSALM 34:18[1]

---

1. NIV

FIVE WORDS

If you approach my house from the rear street, before reaching the yard you can see through the trees to my back door. Normally, I don't pay attention. I've never actually stopped and searched through those trees—not until this past week.

Now I care.

As soon as I reach the rear street, my heart fills with hope. I stop my vehicle and hastily scan the area. Just as quickly, sadness darkens my expectation. He's not there.

Tiglath-pileser IV, my eight-month-old kitten, has been missing for the past week. It feels like months. He's solid black, neutered.

The first night, I suspected something very wrong had happened—I know my pet. Tiglath kept a Ronald Reagan presidential routine: up at five, returning midday for a nap, back at nine for bedtime.

Friends assured me he'd return.

"He's off with his buddies," one said.

Except his feline pals still arrive each morning, looking for him. Less often, now.

The first night I was out at two in the morning, searching a wide radius around my house, certain I'd find him dead in the street. That didn't happen, thankfully.

But something got him.

I'm a live-and-let-live kind of person. I wonder now if I should have been more cautious. Something had tunneled into my yard, and I wonder if that something got him. Friday, for the first time in my life, I had pest control come. They took charge of that hole.

You learn in seminary that one death raises another.

I found myself thinking of my parents this week. I sat in my car crying yesterday, uncertain just who I was grieving for. My kitten, yes —but also for those I've dearly loved and lost.

I wanted to write about sorrow months ago. Teri Youhanaie, my friend of three decades, had called to tell me of her dad's passing. He'd had a stroke and had been severely disabled for years. Her mom—this strong, devout, amazing woman—had cared for him all that time. She's one of a kind.

The funeral was on the West Coast, and I called the next morning. "I hope your dad's service went well."

"It was beautiful," she said, "but my mom passed in her sleep in the night."

As I write this, I can hear her weeping—something I'd never heard before. She's blonde with a sunny disposition. Her tears were the sound of clean, pure grief.

I'm well-educated, but I never know what to say. At some point, I shared words I hold dear: "The Lord is close to the brokenhearted . . ."[1]

I wanted to write something for her, but I told another friend, "All I can think of is the obvious."

Yesterday, as I was grieving, this second friend said to me, "The Lord is your shepherd."

Five words.

And the "obvious" brought me so much comfort.

If you are a person of faith, you'll know what that Psalm says:

"The Lord is my shepherd, I shall not want. He makes me lie down

---

1. Psalm 34:18 NIV

in green pastures. He leads me beside still waters. He restores my soul."[2]

I found myself adding Jesus' words:

". . . my peace I give to you."[3]

"Come to Me, all who are weary and heavy-laden, and I will give you rest."[4]

Loss can affect one deeply—it's readjusting your life to the void. If you love profoundly, it takes time. The larger the abyss, the longer it may be.

Norman Vincent Peale said to memorize Scripture, that it would bubble up and care for you in time of need. It will.

The Lord is your shepherd. He is close to the brokenhearted.

---

2. Psalm 23:1-3 ESV
3. John 14:27 ESV
4. Matthew 11:28 NASB

Notes, Revelation, Prayers
Date:_____

If God moved in your heart, record your notes, revelation, prayers.

16

HEBREWS

BSB TIME

". . . let us run with endurance the race that is set before us . . ."

HEBREWS 12:1[1]

---

1. ESV

BSB TIME

The moon is high in the sky as they make their way through the darkness, shivering from the cold, navigating empty streets. Each moves silently toward a vacant room in the basement of a large building. They have come for decades—one day each week. None has ever left this group, except by death.

They are not alone.

Many such groups meet elsewhere. They quietly gather, unbeknownst to most. They talk of blood and human sacrifice.

I know for a fact there's such a group in my town.

Ten men.

Yes.

I knew one of them. Actually, I knew him pretty well. I suspected he might be involved in such a matter—but I didn't know for sure.

On a fateful day, months ago, this man called me over to his table at lunch. Another man sat there.

Innocently, I joined them. I could never have expected what was about to happen.

The man I knew quietly introduced the other man, told me about their meetings, and asked whether I'd come.

Oh, I had an easy out. I could have said that the time of day would be impossible.

But, no. Forget that. I decided to go.

Days later, I stumbled from my house into blackness—a full moon high in the sky—and braved those cold, dark, empty streets.

At a quarter before six in the morning, I stepped to the door of that basement and walked inside. After this first meeting, they asked me to join them.

I told this story to several people, wondering what they'd think.

"Witches," the first replied.

"The KKK," another said.

It's a Baptist men's Bible study.

This account is how Romans and Jews saw the early church. What we easily understand as communion and Christ's crucifixion, they thought were rituals of drinking blood and sacrificing humans. Such confusion contributed to hostility and persecution against the early church.

Some Christians—faced with losing their property, homes, and even their lives—fearfully decided to leave the risen Lord.

The letter to the Hebrews addressed this crisis, emphasizing the importance of joining together: "Consider how we may spur one another on . . . not giving up meeting together . . . but encouraging one another."[1]

This need is as strong today as ever.

We face enormous pressure to "get with the times" and leave the commandments of God. Every Christian should attend church and find a small Bible study. We are stronger together.

When I walked into that church basement, my friend wasn't there to introduce me. Only a few men had arrived, and they sat together at a table for 10. I recognized one and smiled, maybe with a wave. I can't remember exactly.

Obviously, I was faced with "group dynamics." Yes, you know

---

1. Hebrews 10:24-25, NIV

what I mean. Imagine showing up for church and another family having taken your pew.

"We thought we'd change it up," they say.

You stand there nodding with your mouth hanging open, wanting to say, "It's MY pew!"

That's group dynamics.

I knew this pre-crack-of-dawn Bible study had met for decades. So, clearly, each man had his seat. If I had been alert, I would have asked where to sit. But, no, my brain moves on turtle legs at a quarter 'til six, inching along, and I just sat down.

I didn't know at the time that one of the 10 often couldn't attend. What are the odds I'd pick his seat? Ten to one, right? Ten percent chance.

Now, add in the possibility that I would also pick the seat beside my thoughtful friend, who still hadn't arrived to introduce me. I'm guessing less than a one percent chance I would get that right.

Obviously, that didn't happen.

But it did.

Defying the odds, I chose the usually vacant seat, and it was right beside my friend's!

Impossible. But not with the Lord. He sayeth, "Oh, snap!" God made clear His position: "This is where you belong!"

The Lord talks to us.

The message may come as words you actually hear or from a feeling. It may come from a dream, through people, from a Scripture passage, or during incidents like this. Perhaps there's a message to you right now as you read these words.

Join a small Bible study. You will love your BSBs—Bible Study Buddies. These folks will be with you in sorrow and joy.

A friend of mine treasures her Bible study group. "A wonderful benefit," she said, "is the relationships you develop—getting a group who will pray for you. These are the people I emailed from the hospital when my dad was dying."

My BSBs strengthen me in my walk with Jesus. "Iron sharpens iron."[2]

We all need this.

Scripture tells us plainly: ". . . lay aside every encumbrance and the sin which so easily entangles us, and let us run with endurance the race that is set before us."[3]

As I said, pre-dawn Bible studies are not just in my town. Across the world, the moon is high in the sky as Christians make their way through the darkness, shivering from the cold, navigating empty streets. Such study times also happen at noon, in the evening, and on Saturdays. In every instance, these Christians are determined to do as Scripture says, "Consider how we may spur one another on . . . not giving up meeting together . . . but encouraging one another."[4]

Prayerfully consider what God is saying to you right now. A Bible study group should be a part of every Christian's life.

2. Proverbs 27:17, NASB
3. Hebrews 12:1, NASB
4. Hebrews 10:24-25, NIV

Notes, Revelation, Prayers   Date:_____

If God moved in your heart, record your notes, revelation, prayers.

17

BARTIMAEUS

WHAT GOD PLACES ON YOUR HEART

"God has not given us a spirit of fear . . . but of power . . ."

2 TIMOTHY 1:7[1]

---

1. NLT

WHAT GOD PLACES ON YOUR HEART

My Aunt Elizabeth was five years old when she destroyed her mother, my grandmother.

Elizabeth, the youngest of nine children, knew whose turn it was to say grace. It didn't matter that her mother had invited the preacher and his wife for dinner, it was still her turn.

She displayed great reverence, her hands folded in prayer on her plate, her chubby legs dangling quietly beneath the table.

"Jesus, thank you for this food!" she stated loudly.

The preacher, thinking little Elizabeth had finished, lifted his head, eyed my grandmother, and nodded his approval.

"And, Jesus," Elizabeth continued, "please don't bless nobody but us!"

Elizabeth's "me and mine" stage was quickly corrected. My grandmother earnestly believed in generosity toward others.

Jesus also confronted "me and mine" selfishness as He was leaving Jericho one day. Surrounded by a great crowd moving along with Him, Jesus abruptly stopped and said, "Call him here."

Call whom?

Jesus didn't say. He didn't have to, everyone knew.

Bartimaeus, a blind man, had been sitting by the road begging when he heard the throng moving toward him and realized it was the Lord. So, Bartimaeus cried out, "Jesus, Son of David, have mercy on me!"

Despite the multitude, who must have been clamoring for Jesus' attention, the Lord stopped and focused on this blind man.

Why?

Bartimaeus had become a spectacle.

The blind man had seen his chance to be healed and kept shouting to Jesus to have mercy on him. But that wasn't the all of it. There was more that made this scene an event—and not a good one.

Those in the crowd near Bartimaeus had begun trying to silence the blind beggar. Mind you, it wasn't just a few telling Bartimaeus to be quiet. Scripture says there were "many." Here's the passage.

". . . as (Jesus) was leaving Jericho with His disciples and a large crowd, a beggar who was blind named Bartimaeus, the son of Timaeus, was sitting by the road. And when he heard that it was Jesus the Nazarene, he began to cry out and say, 'Jesus, Son of David, have mercy on me!' *Many* were sternly telling him to be quiet, but he kept crying out all the more, 'Son of David, have mercy on me!'"[1]

If you look closely at the passage, you will see that there's even more going on than the group trying to silence the blind man. Every version of this story I've read is almost identical, but at this place in the narrative they diverge. The version I just quoted, the New American Standard Bible, says the silencers spoke "sternly" to Bartimaeus. Another version says they "rebuked" the man. A third says they *warned him.*

The people warned him?

Were those near Bartimaeus threatening this blind man for yelling to Jesus for help? Did he face a beating if he didn't quiet down?

What else can a warning mean?

The threats didn't faze the blind man. Bartimaeus kept shouting, longing for Jesus to heal him.

See? A spectacle.

---

1. Mark 10:46-48, NASB (emphasis added)

But why did this happen?

The Bible abounds with people bringing the sick and handicapped to the Lord. Why didn't someone help blind Bartimaeus through the crowd to Jesus?

Maybe because the other healings were the "me and mine" kind—my family, my servants, my friends.

Bartimaeus, however, was alone. A beggar. And the "me and mine" folks were not about to let him get ahead of them.

This story is painful to read, much less to have experienced. But there was Jesus, watching it unfold.

So, the Lord said, "Call him."

I love this part. Love it!

Our Lord didn't step through the crowd to the man or send the disciples for him. Usually He did one or the other. Instead, Jesus spoke to the crowd. Deliberately, Jesus said, "Call him here."

You know what that meant.

Those next to Bartimaeus, the "me and mine" folks, the ones threatening him, had to tell the blind man that the Lord wanted him.

Scripture relays what happened when those people were put on the spot. Here it is:

"And when he heard that it was Jesus the Nazarene, he began to cry out and say, 'Jesus, Son of David, have mercy on me!' Many were sternly telling him to be quiet, but he kept crying out all the more, 'Son of David, have mercy on me!' And Jesus stopped and said, 'Call him here.' So they called the man who was blind, saying to him, 'Take courage, stand up! He is calling for you.'"[2]

Did you see that?

The crowd changed—now they're saying, "Take courage, stand up! He is calling for you."

It's just amazing.

Understand that this blind beggar was not otherwise handicapped nor was he an old man. Scripture tells us what Bartimaeus did upon

---

2. Mark 10:46-49, NASB

hearing Jesus' words. "And throwing off his cloak, (Bartimaeus) jumped up and came to Jesus."[3]

But how did this blind man get through the large crowd? How did he find Jesus?

Watch me grin.

Those beside the blind beggar, the selfish mean-spirited ones, the people who had warned him, were now forced not just to celebrate that the Lord wanted the beggar, but to lead Bartimaeus to Jesus.

The Lord then asked him directly. "What do you want me to do for you?"

"Rabbi, I want to see," he said.

And Jesus healed him immediately. "Go, your faith has made you well."[4]

When Jesus was in His hometown, He couldn't perform many miracles because the people didn't believe.[5] But Bartimaeus believed, and he was healed.

Do not miss God's message in this story. If Bartimaeus hadn't kept yelling, if he'd given up, if he'd cowered under the crowd's cruelty, Bartimaeus would have lived and died a blind beggar.

But the man kept crying out to get the Lord's attention, willing to risk any humiliation and all danger. "Jesus, Son of David, have mercy on me!" he shouted louder and louder.

Do the same. Do not give up!

Jesus shamed the crowd that day, but know that those people live on. They'll fight you, trying to instill fear in you as they did with Bartimaeus. You aren't going to get ahead of them, not if they can help it. They act from selfishness, rivalry, jealousy.

Don't listen to them.

The biggest naysayer may be yourself, thinking you aren't good enough for the new opportunity, the new house, the new relationship. We shush our yearning and walk away, refusing to try.

---

3. Mark 10:50, NASB
4. Mark 10:52, NASB
5. Matthew 13:58

"No one is going to publish this," I said after writing my first newspaper article. Had it been left to me, I'd have thrown it away.

But I had promised a man I owed a favor, so I submitted that article. Then my first editor published it and kept publishing my pieces, believing in me. Otherwise, I would not have become a faith columnist. Truly, writing alongside God each week is amazing.

When I first edited this in 2017, most newspapers did not want words about Jesus. Thankfully, I was guided to one that did.

If God places something on your heart, seize the opportunities that come. You disappoint Him if you say, "I can't—"

Let me repeat that: You disappoint God if you say, "I can't—"

Little Elizabeth's "me and mine" self-centeredness and the crowd's selfishness were both quickly corrected. Bartimaeus received healing because of his faith, but also because he kept yelling to Jesus.

Be as strong as that blind man.

"God has not given us a spirit of fear . . . but of power . . ." [6]

---

6. 2 Timothy 1:7, NLT

Notes, Revelation, Prayers Date:_____

If God moved in your heart, record your notes, revelation, prayers.

PART II

GUIDANCE FROM GOD

18

WHERE IT ALL BEGAN

STRANDED IN THE DEEP SOUTH

"My Presence will go with you, and I will give you rest."

EXODUS 33:14[1]

---

1. NIV

STRANDED IN THE DEEP SOUTH

Author's note:

This is the first article I wrote for a newspaper. Before this, I had won small awards for fiction, and I had no interest in writing nonfiction. But I did it, as I said in the last chapter, because I owed a man a favor—the marvelous Preston Boutwell, whom you will meet later in this book. That was all he wanted.

I had no idea about the proper word count for a newspaper article, and this chapter is a lot longer than others in the book. In fact, the article was so large that it took up most of the little town's once-a-week newspaper. I should say half of it took up most of that newspaper. They had to run it over two weeks!

I take seriously the words of Proverbs 11:14: "...in the abundance of counselors there is victory." In other words, I really listened to my editors when I wrote this book.

However, they were at opposite ends of the spectrum on how much of this article to include. Some said to leave it completely intact, while others felt it needed to be shorter. I did edit it heavily from the original, but it's still a good deal longer than the rest of the chapters.

Here it is. Where it all began. Feel free to skim.

When this woman starts a 1,000-mile road trip, she thinks of Ted Bundy or those Cleveland women held in captivity. The Friday before Memorial Day in 2015, I began just such a trip from deep in the South, heading north. I wasn't sure how long I'd be gone—I packed winter clothes, if that gives you any idea.

I have two vehicles: my mom's Cadillac with 100,000 miles and a Jeep, 10 years older, with 250,000 miles. Obviously, the Cadillac was the better choice.

Obviously.

I had taken it to my local mechanic who had given me a thumbs up. Even so, as I drove north, that vehicle started talking to me and not in a good way. It was sick. It sputtered.

Okay, but just how sick are you?

I kept going, hoping she was overreacting. It was just the sniffles, a cold starting for a few of those two hundred horses under her hood.

Before long, the engine began fighting me—it had a fever. Something very serious was going on.

Stubborn, I kept going, certain it wasn't that serious, certain the mechanic would have known, certain he wouldn't have let me start on this trip in an unsafe vehicle.

Finally, the Cadillac threatened to die, warning me over and over again. The engine was not getting fuel, or at least it felt like that. I looked at my mileage indicator—I had driven less than 100 miles.

How can this be happening?

I pulled off the road at the first station and started hearing beeping. Was this my vehicle? It now sounded like a bomb about to explode. I looked around and frowned. It seemed as though it was the station, but that was crazy—gas stations don't beep.

"Out of business!" a man yelled from the house next door. Apparently, the beeping had something to do with the station's status.

It was probably the hottest day of the year, and he sat back in the shadows of his garage. I walked toward him gingerly, hoping he wasn't related to Ted.

Bundy, that is.

I explained about the car trouble, eyeing his small "Boiled Peanuts for Sale" sign. *Seriously? On the hottest day of the year?*

Then I turned and eyed the road.

Clearly, the man had more than one problem with his sales platform. His house sat way back from the highway—anyone passing at a clip wouldn't have noticed him or his house, much less his little sign.

"Just go down to the Texaco at the light," he said. "Best mechanic in town!"

He gave me long, detailed directions.

"Okay," I said, paying no attention.

How big can this little town be?

At the first light, I realized the city was a bit larger than I had anticipated. I remembered him saying something about a hill and the left side of the road. I turned the corner and searched.

No hill. No Texaco, left or right.

The town had only three stoplights. There wasn't a Texaco at any of them. I wandered around in circles until I finally stopped and asked again.

"You passed it," the next man said. "Best mechanic in town. Right there!"

So I backtracked, paying a lot more attention to the second set of directions. Still, no Texaco.

I stopped again. "Where EXACTLY is it?"

I followed those directions to a tee. No Texaco. I did see a "Service Center" and eyed the tower in front as I pulled in. It looked like it might have once been a sign.

"Is this the Texaco?" I asked.

"Used to be," the man said.

I smiled. *No, sir, it still is.*

The first mechanic, the one in Florida who had given me the thumbs up, had also put in a new compressor, new hose, and new Freon. So at least I had just driven those 100 miles on the hottest day of the year in a cool vehicle. Right?

Wrong.

The air didn't work either.

I retreated inside the service center, sweating profusely—that area was cooler than outside. A man followed after me. He had seen my distress and turned on a window air conditioner.

Do I look that bad? Probably.

A nice woman asked if I needed an appointment for next week.

"I'm not going to be here next week," I said, alarm in my voice. "I'm just passing through, headed north. Can someone look at my vehicle now?"

Everyone dropped everything and came to my aid. I was grateful. Even more grateful to be in the hands of the "best mechanic in town." That was the unanimous opinion on my pilgrimage to the not-Texaco: no better mechanic anywhere.

The best mechanic in town didn't take long to return. Something about a torque—I didn't pay attention. What I heard was the part about him not being able to fix it.

You're kidding? The best mechanic in town? You can't fix it?

He sent me down the road to another place, saying he took his vehicle there. Okay, I really, really liked that part. I am now off to the best-mechanic-in-town's mechanic. Good hands, right?

I listened closely to the directions and followed them to a tee. No sign anywhere. I did see several large garages and a smaller building with many vehicles parked outside.

Is this the place?

There wasn't a soul in sight.

I got out, swiping at sweat on my brow. Why did I think there would be a sign—some words somewhere that mentioned Automotive Repair? Why did I think that?

I walked toward the buildings gingerly.

Anybody in captivity in there?

You never know.

Fairly quickly, a man emerged from the garage. He seemed safe enough, so I recounted my tale—the engine fighting me, the not-Texaco guy saying something about a torque, the 1,000-mile trip ahead.

He said there was no way he could fix it, that he'd be working late finishing what he had on hand. He told me no one was going to be open anywhere on Memorial Day weekend.

"If you find a place," he continued, "you really wouldn't want them working on your car."

The man didn't look like a sage, but there was truth in those words. He said he wasn't coming back to work until Tuesday.

"Can you please just look at it?" I asked.

"No."

"You can't even tell me if you can fix it on Tuesday? I don't want to wait four days if you can't fix it."

"No."

He gave me a reason, something about codes and this and that. I couldn't listen—all I could think about was being stranded in a tiny Southern town for four whole days. Worse yet, the acute realization hit me that on Tuesday morning the best-mechanic-in-town's mechanic might not be able to fix my vehicle. Actually, I'm pretty sure he said this.

"You could go to Enterprise," he added.

"You want me to rent a car?"

"Enterprise is a city. A few hours—"

"Tuesday," I said. "I'll be back."

I made a very fast executive decision—for me, this is quite rare. I didn't know anyone in Enterprise, and it was far away. I wasn't even certain I could get there. This guy already had more recommendations than anyone I could possibly find in such a short space of time. I wanted him.

I drove around the corner and checked into the local hotel. The rate gagged me. *You get that here?*

The woman smiled and made me a better deal.

It's dinner time now—what the Deep South calls *supper.* Good thing we drifted to this topic because that can cause you trouble. Like when someone says, "Come by after dinner," and you go at 6 p.m., but they expected you after lunch.

I know this for a fact, having shown up wayyy too late for an event.

I returned to the downtown area to the only people I know—my new besties at the not-Texaco. I drove beside the pump and pulled out my credit card to get gas. No slot. I went inside.

"How much do you want?" she asked.

"I have no idea." I waved the credit card midair, as if to explain. "There's always a slot."

She nodded toward the pump, the pump closest to the road. "Just go ahead and get it."

Seriously?

So I did, wondering when I'd last bought gas without paying for it first. Gas by the road, no less. Well, let's see—not in this decade, probably not in this century.

I returned and handed her my card, still sweating. "All set!" I said, proud of adjusting so quickly to small-town living.

"How much did you get?"

I stared at her. *I'm supposed to know this?*

Before I could reach for the door, her husband dashed outside and right back with the amount.

They gave me a list of the local eating establishments, pointing this way and that. I wrote down the names, wondering if any of them would have a sign.

What does one do on a long weekend in a little Southern town while waiting on car repairs? I found out. I went and looked at the highly recommended lake. Nice lake. The part about the island and a picnic sounded wonderful—that is, until the man at the gate mentioned the 11 alligators.

"They won't hurt you," he said.

I knew why he added that part. I get a certain look when I think of Ted Bundy or the trapped Cleveland women. Sheer fear. I'll now call it my 11-alligator look.

"There was that one time," he continued.

"What one time?"

"No one got hurt."

"What one time?"

"A man was swimming," he said, "and an alligator chased him, but he didn't bite him or anything."

Or anything?

That's supposed to make me feel better!

I kept thinking about those 11 wise alligators, eating people whole —no witnesses, no evidence.

The island picnic was now a definite no.

I actually tried to get to a larger, nearby town, but the car threatened to die over and over again.

Fortunately, I do carry every manner of electronic gadget and worked part of the weekend. I tried several restaurants.

You have to remember this was supposed to be a two-day trip. My vehicle was packed to the gills for my indefinite stay up North. I had left out two sundresses, which was all I thought I needed.

Did I want to go digging through my car for clothes? No. So I wore those two dresses. I didn't know anyone in town—what difference did it make?

Where I was living in Florida, everyone dressed just like I do. I didn't see one sundress in this town. No one looked anything like I do. Just as an aside, *everyone* I met goes to church, just like I do.

The church part felt amazing! Simply amazing!

For reasons I cannot explain, I started looking at the real estate listings online. I like interesting, historic homes and eyed three.

While I was out wandering around, I suddenly heard myself say, "If I could find a house with this one rare feature, I might buy it." After all, the town wasn't far from where I lived in Florida. I could escape the summer craziness and also protect my precious belongings from hurricanes.

As I roamed that weekend, I passed all three of those houses. My jaw dropped—this was also amazing. I couldn't quite believe that every house online was right there, blocks apart.

Okay, fair to say I wasn't used to small-town living.

At all.

Get ready for this: Lo and behold, one of the three houses had that rare feature I wanted!

I stopped my car and stared.

Not possible!

Fate? Synchronicity? God? What? I mean, what are the chances? And when you find such a rare feature, those homes are never for sale.

I got out of my car and approached the house, unsure if it was occupied. One would hate to get caught peeking into the windows where a person lives—I'm also pretty certain it's a crime. I kept circling the house on foot, moving closer and closer until I was sure it was empty. Then I peered into one room after another, nose to the glass.

What a charming, old house!

It's now the Sunday before Memorial Day, and I called a close friend and told him about the house.

"Have you lost your marbles!" he shouted. "You cannot stop in a little town and buy a house!"

That did not dissuade me. I explained how I really hated the idea of keeping my grandmother's prayer table on a barrier island.

"No, No, No!" he continued. "NO!"

I went back and looked at the house.

The man across the street was an unbelievable sign. (I love signs and wonders—I live for them.) He's not only the associate minister at the Baptist church, he also has the most gorgeous yard. And I'm not even at the unbelievable part. Not yet. Here it comes: My dog, Baby, decided his yard, with him standing there watching, was the best place in the world to poop.

"I'll get that!" I quickly said, having been scolded more than once for Baby's poor judgment.

"It's good for the ground," he said.

"It is?" I grinned. *Yes, I want you for my neighbor!*

He directed me to the next block down, telling me about Ms. Libby.

"It was her parents' house," he said. "She knows all about it."

I trooped right down there. Even so, I knew not everyone wants their day interrupted by an adventurous soul. Right away, I saw the sign by the door and felt certain I was in good hands. It read, "As for me and my house, we shall serve the Lord."

I rang the doorbell. A woman appeared, looking at me quizzically.

"Are you Ms. Libby?" I asked.

Immediately, the biggest smile imaginable filled her face. "I am."

She and her husband settled into the porch swing and told me all about the charming, old house.

Did I mention this part—I love the people in this little town!

"I'm going to take you to church with us," her husband said.

I have lived in my much larger Florida town for many years, and no one had ever invited me to church. Not once. Nada.

I actually took one of my electronic gadgets and listened to their minister. Isn't the electronic age something? You can go back in time and listen to a sermon that happened weeks ago in your hotel room with a few taps of a finger.

I liked what he had to say. Unlike my listening skills with mechanics, I pay attention to ministers. I know what's what, and he did a fine job.

David Ellis showed me the house on Memorial Day. I had nothing else to do. I feel certain he had plenty happening—a day scheduled to the max with family events. But I told him if, miracle of miracles, my car was ready to go on Tuesday morning, I was heading north immediately. I didn't want to go north at all, but there were things to do. Pressing things.

"This may be the only day I have to see it," I told David.

Remember, I had no A/C and Baby was sick. I didn't want her in the heat, so I asked if we could go "early." Seven a.m. early.

We did. David Ellis proved to be the sweetest, most flexible, laid-back realtor ever—wonderful man!

As I drifted deeper and deeper into the house, I began doing the math. "It needs some work," I said. "The expensive kind."

Actually, I said a lot more, but I won't bore you with the details.

I went to the local diner after that and asked if the town was a safe place to live. Of course, it is. I get that now, but on day three I had no idea. One of the waitresses actually knew the woman who had owned the house after Ms. Libby. Why does that not surprise me?

Someone recommended the restaurant's cheesecake. Uh, yes, the cheesecake is wonderful. I need to stay away from the diner.

On Tuesday, I was up at 5 a.m.—D-day for my car. I called what I thought was my mechanic, and an elegant British woman on the voice recording asked me to leave a message.

What?

"Uh—" I said and stopped, certain I had the wrong number. I left a message anyway, reminding him of our conversation on Friday.

Immediately, I went by his place. Did he start at six? Seven?

No.

Also, no sign indicating the hours of operation. Why did that not surprise me? I stuck a note under the door with my name and number, reminding him who I was.

I also called him from breakfast at the diner. Yes, my mind was swirling, wondering if he was even going to have time to diagnose it on Tuesday. He answered and told me to come at 9:30. I am never early for anything. Never.

I was there at 9:20.

As I sat in his office, one person after another came with their cars and sob stories—why did that all sound so familiar? Oh yes, they were just like me. He patiently listened as they poured out their troubles and then told them next week.

The man underestimated his ability to decipher my problem. He knew within minutes and quickly made a phone call. I listened; it sounded dire. It was.

To paraphrase, my Cadillac was bad news back when it was birthed. He told me a lot of mechanical things which I didn't understand. The bottom line: Don't take it anywhere.

I have to take it. I have to get there!

"Can you make it better?" I said.

"Yes."

"Let's go with that."

He ordered some parts—estimated time of arrival Thursday. He also looked at the A/C and said there wasn't a drop of Freon in it. That didn't surprise me. He put in dye and coolant. Thankfully, I was cool again.

Something made me call him later that afternoon. Was it:

(a) Jesus;

(b) My guardian angel;

(c) The Holy Spirit; or

(d) All of the above?

I'm going with (d).

"I have another vehicle," I said. "It has a quarter of a million miles on it, so . . ."

I waited. Obviously, he was going to tell me to forget it, to take the Cadillac.

He didn't miss a beat. "Anything would be better than that Cadillac."

Are you serious?

I don't think I'd heard a word he'd said until that moment.

Enter the local Exxon. I had learned they would take me anywhere I wanted to go. After a flurry of phone calls with the man at Exxon, we decided to travel hours south and get the Jeep that afternoon.

"I'm on my way into the lot," the man finally said.

"I'm coming!" I grabbed my things and scurried out of the hotel.

No Exxon.

"Where are you?" I said, calling him back. "I thought you were in the lot."

"No, I said I was on my way out of the lot."

"Where are you now?"

"On my way out of the lot."

You gotta love small-town life. But, to be fair, consonants can be pretty soft or lost altogether in a deep Southern drawl. You have to pay attention.

Exxon arrived with a humongous vehicle. I opened the door and stared up at the steep climb.

"Little old ladies can get in here," he said.

I nodded. *Okay, then. No little old lady is going to best me. Not today, anyway.*

I hoisted Baby into the seat, lifted my full-length sundress, and climbed those steep steps to where even the elderly can go.

"I saw you in the diner yesterday," Preston Boutwell said right off, before we had even left the hotel lot. I looked down at my clothes and winced.

In this.

I had an awakening at that moment—in this town where everyone knew everyone else, I stood out. One and only one thing flashed across my mind: *I have to break out a suitcase!*

"Does the Jeep run?" he asked.

"Yes, but it needs new tires."

"I'll make you a good deal!"

I see. Preston owns Exxon.

When you travel four hours round trip with a person, you get to know them. I told Preston my life story, and he told me his. We told jokes. We shared our joys and our tragedies. We talked about the Bible —my great love, as if you didn't know. His favorite character (other than Jesus) is Paul. Mine is David. He likes the Gospels the best. I love the Gospels, too. I also treasure the Old Testament, love those stories.

I warned him that my Jeep was in storage with boxes of junk all around it. I told him there were about five, and I'd have to stuff that stuff in the Jeep. I didn't want to pay a huge storage bill for a few boxes.

Fine with him.

When we arrived, it was obvious I had remembered this wrong— there were a lot more than five boxes.

Preston treated me like kinfolk and grabbed one box after another, fishing stuff out and shoving it into that SUV. It was amazing.

Believe me, not many people would have done that.

It was also hot, really hot. We were both sweating, and I felt terrible, but he acted like it was absolutely nothing. It wore me out. Preston, who could retire if he wanted to, didn't look a bit scathed.

Preston has a son who works with him, Little Preston. Preston keeps in touch with people who go way back. He lives for football games and enjoys them with the same couples. He eats every morning with men from his church. He's lived in that small town all his life. I'd say he has a good life.

We arrived back in the little metropolis that evening and dropped the Jeep off to get it repaired. I went by first thing on Wednesday morning and cleaned out enough stuff so a human could get behind the wheel.

Yes, it was that full.

Then I waited for the verdict from the best-mechanic-in-town's mechanic. I thought for certain I'd have to take the parts he'd ordered for the Cadillac (I'd already paid for them).

But he had somehow canceled that.

He looked at the Jeep, called me, and was elated that he could make it all work for the same price he'd quoted me on the Cadillac.

Meanwhile, I had nothing to do for most of Wednesday and began circling that historic house. The police stopped twice and gave me a good once-over. I loved that! An interested police force is a great thing!

I called my friend back. "I'm going to make an offer."

"No, you're not!" he said. "No! No! NO!"

I made the offer.

On Thursday, I had to check out of the hotel at noon. My car wouldn't be ready until five, so I pretty much lounged around the auto place with nowhere else to go.

"Great location," I said.

He's right at the corner of three major highways. Inevitably, the land will be in demand, and when that happens, he plans to sell and retire.

He's not an old man.

"What are you going to do when you retire?" I asked.

It didn't take him long to answer. "Open a little repair shop somewhere."

I smiled. Isn't that the essence of contentment—to love what you're doing so much you'd continue if you had all the money in the world? I saw that in both Preston and David. They love what they do.

Me too!

Of course, it had to storm that afternoon. At five, after transferring all my belongings from one vehicle to the other in the rain and mud, I hurried to the Exxon. I had already priced the tires for my Jeep and

Preston was good to his word—he made me a great deal. I rolled in and his men set to work like a well-oiled machine. I am not kidding! Fifteen minutes later I was rolling out!

Why were people so nice to me?

Could it be that I had simply landed in a nice town? It almost felt like these people came from that long-ago era when honor meant more than money. They knew I needed help and wanted to help me.

I finished my trip north on Saturday night. Nice tires, nice ride.

Did the best-mechanic-in-town's mechanic keep me safe from the hands of the Ted Bundys of the world? Definitely.

As for David Ellis—did I buy that house? Let me say these words from God: "My Presence will go with you, and I will give you rest."[1]

I made multiple offers on the house for two months. All of them were refused. The next chapter is a big-fish tale you must read to understand how the story ends.

And it's regular length.

---

1. Exodus 33:14, NIV

Notes, Revelation, Prayers   Date:_____
If God moved in your heart, record your notes, revelation, prayers.

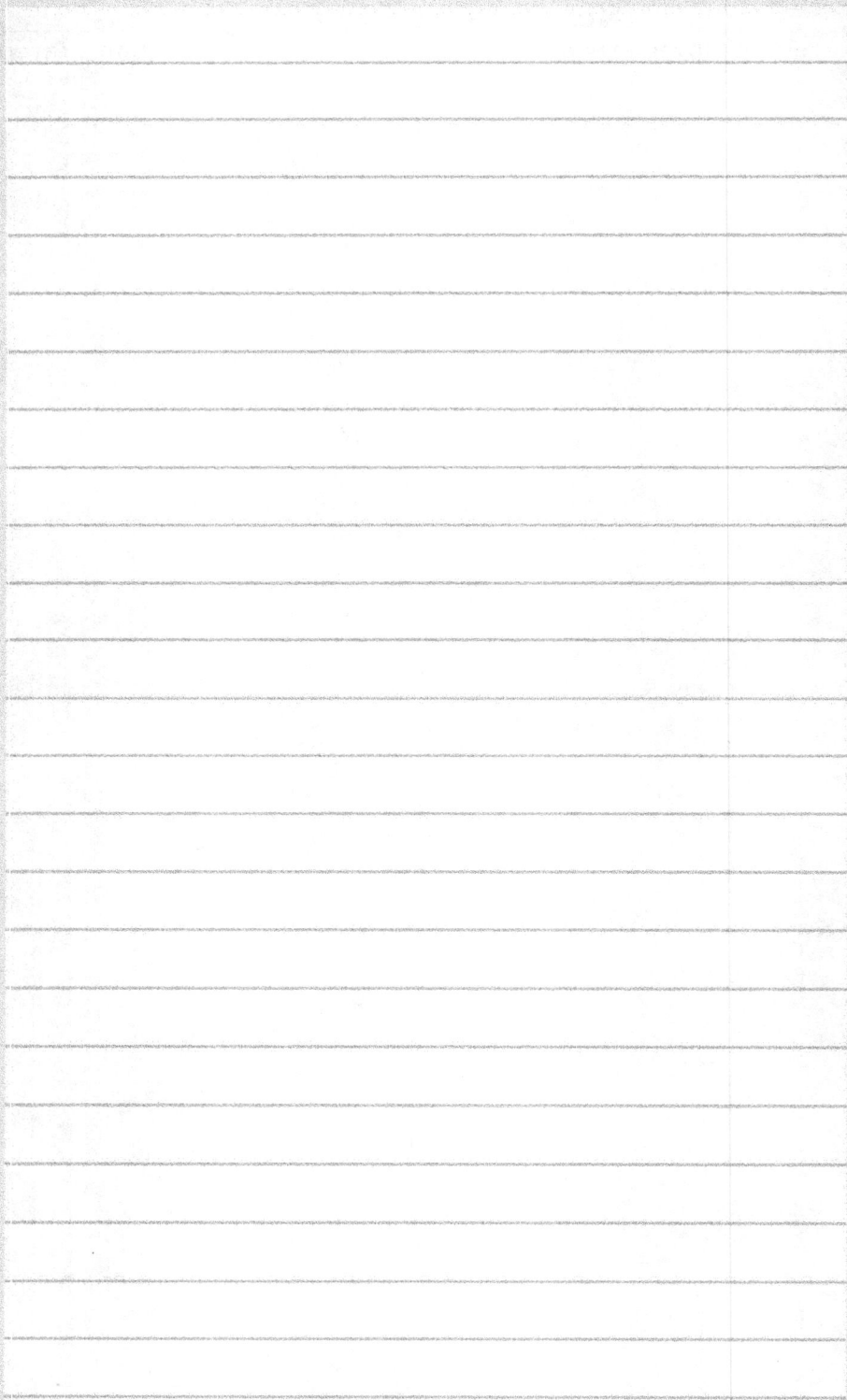

19

MIRACLES MUST BE REMEMBERED

A BIG-FISH TALE

"... do not forget the things your eyes have seen ..."

DEUTERONOMY 4:9[1]

---

1. NIV

A BIG-FISH TALE

There are big-fish tales. You know what I mean, highly unlikely stories—the kind that cause old men to yell, "Balderdash!"

This is one of them.

In fact, I wouldn't have the pluck to tell it, but there are witnesses. Living ones.

My big-fish tale begins the week before Memorial Day, when I was hurrying north on a dreaded road trip—the one I wrote about previously in Chapter 18. My mother's red Cadillac decided to break down near a small town, and the best mechanic there waved me down the road to his mechanic. After a week of drama, I switched vehicles, and then safely made the trip north in my Jeep.

However, before I could leave, I had to transfer all my belongings from one vehicle to the other—each one just as stuffed as before, but my necessities were now in the Jeep and the rest filled the Caddy. Mind you, every day I'd spent in that town had been hot and sunny. Now, it started to storm.

At five o'clock, quitting time, my mechanic stepped toward his garage door. By now, I was soaked to the bone and still stuffing my Jeep. Even so, I saw him hesitate, glancing up at the door, then down toward the opening.

"Can I help you?" he asked, eyeing my totes, the ones that had somehow wandered inside his garage, making it impossible for him to go home.

"Yes." I was tired

He loaded the remaining items, shifting things so I could see.

I stepped back, grateful for the aid. "I wish I could say this sort of thing never happens to me," I said, swiping at the rain dripping from my chin, feeling thick mud squishing through my sandals. "But it happens all the time."

"When I was eight," he said, shutting the door of the Jeep, "my mom told me I prayed to God for patience." He paused and then turned and moved away. "You shouldn't pray to God for patience."

"You shouldn't?" That was odd. Patience is a fruit of the Spirit. I long to be more patient. "Why not?"

"Because," he said, "God will send you calamity."

I looked around, wondering what he meant, and then stopped abruptly. *He's talking about me!*

There are people—professionals—who say there are no accidents. They insist that one brings disaster upon oneself.

At moments like these, I tend to agree—I always think I'm at fault. Accordingly, I knew who to blame for my next episode of vehicular failure. It didn't help that this mechanic had said the Jeep would outlast me, that it could go 900,000 miles with regular service.

That's *not* what happened.

I had been up North for about three weeks before returning home, deep in the South.

Did my Jeep die in any of the many states I had passed through? No. Did it die anywhere on those 1,000 miles of interstate I traveled? No. Did it quit near the little town where I had been stranded a week? No, but it did fail.

On June 30, one month after my mom's Cadillac was given last rites, my Jeep died right there, in that same town.

"Balderdash!" you shout.

There are witnesses, I tell you. Living ones!

And the odds. Oh, the odds must be phenomenal.

What are the chances I could ever be stranded again in that same small Southern town, ever in an entire lifetime? Much less twice? Much less with a different vehicle?

As the carnival barker says, "Tighten your belts! This ride gets better!"

Here it is. You don't want to miss this part.

My Jeep didn't break down just anywhere in that town—not on Main Street, not on the highway leading out of town, not even within pushing distance of my automotive mechanic.

Where then?

Every story must have a drumroll, and this is where mine goes. Believe me, it's worth the wait.

My Jeep died at the front door of the automotive repair shop. The front door!

"Balderdash!" you shout.

There are witnesses, I tell you. Living ones!

On that unsuspecting morning, I was headed to see the newspaper editor. I stopped to ask my mechanic a quick question, leaving my Jeep running. As I hurried back toward it, rounding the autos on the lot, the Jeep exploded in a gigantic cloud of steam so thick I couldn't see any part of my vehicle.

Nothing.

At all.

The whole Jeep covered in what looked like dense smoke!

The engine died and water gushed to the ground beneath it.

I am telling you, I wouldn't be penning this now if I had been inside that vehicle—I wouldn't be right for a long time.

I rushed back toward the garage. My mechanic lay full body in the mouth of a mammoth truck.

"Water—" That was all I could say.

"Was the A/C on?"

He hadn't heard the Jeep and kept working. I stood there, my eyes bulging.

"That's normal," he said.

"Come." I still couldn't talk.

He glanced up at me from the engine. "I can't," he said. "Not right this minute."

But he came immediately, probably because of that look I get—the 11-alligator one.

So, the best-mechanic-in-town's mechanic knew exactly what to do. He opened the hood and reached into the engine. A melon-sized part promptly fell into his hand.

"It's your steering," he said, in a slow drawl.

I stared at the part and swallowed hard—I had felt the steering wheel fighting me.

"It-it-it just started," I stammered, thinking of those folks who say there are no accidents. "I put steering fluid in it. I did!"

That was true—I had, but apparently not soon enough.

He didn't answer me. Of course, it was my fault, and I wanted to stomp my foot. I should have checked that fluid, but I never do, and nothing like this has ever happened. I rely on oil changes to catch those problems.

Despite this calamity, by nature I am a grateful person. I told the explosion story around town that afternoon, and more than one person lamented my misfortune.

"Good fortune!" I corrected. "I could have been on the interstate. Imagine what might have happened!"

Indeed, several years ago a friend of mine on a motorcycle skidded to a stop on I-65 in the rain. His bike flew out from under him, and he landed on the pavement. A tractor-trailer rolled over his head.

That's a true and tragic story.

That could have been me. Had my Jeep exploded on the interstate, coming to an abrupt halt, a tractor-trailer could have run right over me, crushing my Jeep like a tin can.

There was silence when I returned to see about my Jeep. My mechanic eyed me.

"I know," I said. "I should have checked the steering fluid."

"It wasn't your fault."

"It wasn't?"

"It was a bracket." He stopped, kept eyeing me, and shook his head. "A stress fracture."

"What?"

"The odds of that—" He looked away.

Apparently, the odds of a stress fracture were even greater than the odds of it happening in that same small town, with a different vehicle, a month apart, and at his doorstep.

Oh, yes. I got the message. God was determined to keep me safe that last day of June and also Memorial Day weekend. I believe that.

But consider these two separate auto failures, both in the same place (neither of them my fault, I must righteously add). Was this a sign? Was I supposed to live in this town?!

Three days earlier, I had told my realtor I had decided against the charming, old house. I had told him to make an offer on another house far away.

I promptly went to see him. We looked at the house again, and I made another offer.

Miracles happen every day. They happen to you and me—our big-fish tales. Is each one the hand of God guiding and directing us?

I believe so.

Moreover, I strive to hold these moments close. I do that for a good reason. Why did the Israelites wander for 40 years? Why were the people of God taken into captivity after the grand reigns of David and Solomon?

They lost faith.

In their fear, suffering, and pride, they turned from God. They sought help and guidance elsewhere.

But how did that happen?

How could those chosen by God have forgotten all the miracles Moses showed to Pharaoh—the locusts, the bloody water, the death of every first-born Egyptian male?

And when they stopped believing in God, how is it that no one shouted, "The Red Sea parted!"? How could they have left God?

But it happened. They forgot.

One of the saddest themes of the Bible is how God's people turned away from Him. The verses are too numerous to count. I will include a passage at the end of this chapter with additional reading.[1]

As I said, the verses are too numerous to count.

Each of us will go through hard times—one does not get through a lifetime without suffering.

But it is the miracles, the unbelievable moments with God, the times when we see Him gently caring for us, confidently guiding us—they make all the difference.

They embolden us.

They make us raise our eyes to heaven. They remind us to fall to our knees.

Remember the big-fish tales. Remember yours, remember those in the Bible. Boldly tell them to your children, your best friends, strangers in humongous trucks who pick up your Jeep.

Write them down in a book!

Big-fish tales from God must be cherished. The Lord reminds us: " . . . do not forget the things your eyes have seen . . ." [2]

1. Nehemiah 9:13-31
   Psalm 78:5-64
   Ezekiel 33:10-29.
2. Deuteronomy 4:9, NIV

Scripture Passage
How the Children of God Found Themselves in Great Trouble
II Kings 17:3-20[1]
[This is a really interesting passage and I wanted you to see it.]

Shalmaneser king of Assyria came up to attack Hoshea, who had been Shalmaneser's vassal and had paid him tribute. But the king of Assyria discovered that Hoshea was a traitor, for he had sent envoys to So king of Egypt, and he no longer paid tribute to the king of Assyria, as he had done year by year. Therefore Shalmaneser seized him and put him in prison. The king of Assyria invaded the entire land, marched against Samaria and laid siege to it for three years. In the ninth year of Hoshea, the king of Assyria captured Samaria and deported the Israelites to Assyria. He settled them in Halah, in Gozan on the Habor River and in the towns of the Medes.

Israel Exiled Because of Sin
[What they did was extraordinary and worth knowing. They set their children on fire to appease gods.]

All this took place because the Israelites had sinned against the Lord their God, who had brought them up out of Egypt from under the power of Pharaoh king of Egypt. They worshiped other gods and followed the practices of the nations the Lord had driven out before them, as well as the practices that the kings of Israel had introduced. The Israelites secretly did things against the Lord their God that were not right.

From watchtower to fortified city they built themselves high places in all their towns. They set up sacred stones and Asherah poles on every high hill and under every spreading tree. At every high place they burned incense, as the nations whom the Lord had driven out

---

1. NIV

before them had done. They did wicked things that aroused the Lord's anger.

They worshiped idols, though the Lord had said, "You shall not do this." The Lord warned Israel and Judah through all his prophets and seers: "Turn from your evil ways. Observe my commands and decrees, in accordance with the entire Law that I commanded your ancestors to obey and that I delivered to you through my servants the prophets."

But they would not listen and were as stiff-necked as their ancestors, who did not trust in the Lord their God.

They rejected his decrees and the covenant he had made with their ancestors and the statutes he had warned them to keep. They followed worthless idols and themselves became worthless. They imitated the nations around them although the Lord had ordered them, "Do not do as they do."

They forsook all the commands of the Lord their God and made for themselves two idols cast in the shape of calves, and an Asherah pole. They bowed down to all the starry hosts, and they worshiped Baal.

They sacrificed their sons and daughters in the fire. They practiced divination and sought omens and sold themselves to do evil in the eyes of the Lord, arousing his anger.

So the Lord was very angry with Israel and removed them from his presence. Only the tribe of Judah was left, and even Judah did not keep the commands of the Lord their God. They followed the practices Israel had introduced.

Therefore the Lord rejected all the people of Israel; he afflicted them and gave them into the hands of plunderers, until he thrust them from his presence.[2]

Additional Reading:

Nehemiah 9:13-31
Psalm 78:5-64
Ezekiel 33:10-29

2. II Kings 17:3-20, NIV

Keep a Miracles Journal

I really cannot stress the importance of keeping a Miracles Journal. Write down all that God has done for you and read from it every day. As He gives you new miracles, promptly add to it. Don't say, "I will never forget that." Write it down.

Big-fish tales from God must be cherished.

The Lord reminds us: " . . . do not forget the things your eyes have seen . . ." [3]

---

3. Deuteronomy 4:9, NIV

Notes, Revelation, Prayers Date:_____

If God moved in your heart, record your notes, revelation, prayers.

20

PRESTON BOUTWELL

MORE THAN FULL SERVICE

"You are the light of the world. A city on a hill cannot be hidden."

Matthew 5:14[1]

"In the same way, let your good deeds shine out for all to see, so that everyone will praise your heavenly Father."

Matthew 5:16[2]

---

1. NIV
2. NLT

MORE THAN FULL SERVICE

He's a robust man with a friendly word for everyone. Stop at his service station and ask Preston Boutwell how he's doing.

"Never had a bad day in my life!" he'll say. You can count on it.

If you read Chapter 18, you'll know Preston and I don't go way back—only to last Memorial Day when calamity brought us together.

We spent hours towing my Jeep to town, my little dog curled up between us. I've liked him ever since.

I didn't realize on that day just how important Preston would become to me.

I was unexpectedly stranded in his town for a solid week. Three months later, I bought a home there. One of the reasons was to give my dog and myself some sanity. My house has a nice yard and dog-friendly neighbors, neither of which we had where we'd lived before.

As I said in Chapter 18, the day I first looked at the house, Baby pooped in the minister's yard across the street. The minister was so very nice about it.

Baby also took a hankering to visiting the house on the corner. "Visiting" isn't exactly the right word—she would step up onto their veranda and make herself at home. I made a point to ask these neighbors if it was okay.

"Sure," they said. They didn't mind. But I am fairly certain their scrambling cats had another point of view.

A stray feline took to following Baby. Granted, my dog was really sick, going to the vet twice a week, so there wasn't much Baby could do about it. The cat would walk inches from Baby's tail. I have no idea why, maybe because he could.

Anyway, it was funny—a tiny parade.

When the local police saw her toddling along in the middle of the street, they showed great restraint. I'd wave, running to get her, and they'd wave back. Such is small-town life.

Baby's health had not been good for some time and continued to deteriorate. By November, the vet started saying bad things—that putting her "to sleep" was coming. I knew he was wrong. On one particular weekend, Baby felt better. We went to the beach, and she ate a nice piece of chicken for breakfast and meat again for lunch. Getting her to eat anything substantial could become my goal for the day, so obviously I was relieved.

Now dogs, even those with permits, are not allowed on this beach at midday. However, I am a particularly lucky person. I count on this.

I had lived on that beach for years and knew how it was patrolled. The sheriff has to cover a good many miles several times a day—the odds were low that he would see us.

So you can see that we were good. Right? Smart me chose the time he would be at lunch.

Five minutes after we settled into the sand, Baby on my lap, he rolled onto the beach in his truck. I held my breath, eyeing him.

Go on. Don't stop. Look the other way. Don't see us.

He did just that, rolling past.

Great, I thought.

But then he stopped. The deputy craned his head backward and frowned at me.

"Strictly speaking," I said, as sweetly as possible, "she isn't on the sand." I'm an attorney, I have a nice grasp on technicalities. I also know the value of a smile and beamed at the lawman.

"Doesn't matter," he said roughly.

I had been rocking Baby, and he eyed her frail body cradled against my breast. It must have touched him.

"You can stay," he said with a sigh. "Just stay put."

We had every intention of "staying put." Baby could stand, but by now she couldn't really walk.

Since we had permission to be there, I lay back against the sand and let her body rest on mine. The surf was gentle, the sky blue, the breeze tender—a glorious day.

That weekend was also one of the saddest for me. My little dog took a turn for the worse when we arrived home and died just before midnight.

I am grateful to God for the joy she brought to my life, grateful she outlived the expectations of vet medicine for years. Even more thankful that she passed quietly by the hand of God and not by an injection.

I am beyond grateful.

The next morning, I found Preston at the local diner—his familiar truck parked outside. He eats breakfast there with his buddies before he heads to work, always sitting at what is affectionately called "The Liar's Table."

I joined them, trying to stay calm, relating the tragedy. Before long, I began crying and then sobbing.

"Can I hire one of your men?" I asked him. "To help me bury her."

I didn't know what he'd say. Clearly, it was a big imposition. He needed his men to run the gas station. But I was beside myself with grief, and she'd been dead for almost 10 hours. I feared her body would begin to smell, and the thought of letting that happen wounded me more deeply than I can say.

I could feel almost a panic starting inside. There I was in a new city with no friends—I didn't know where to turn.

Preston didn't hesitate. "We'll be over there in a little bit."

He arrived with one of his men as promised. I had moved her into the living room—still in her bed, her body covered with a hand towel.

"Will you check her?" I asked Preston. "Check her to be sure."

I had sat with her those ten hours, and she hadn't moved, lying there covered in quiet stillness. Even so, I held out hope, remembering the one-in-a-bazillion person who had returned to life unexpectedly at the funeral home.

"Check her," I asked, waving him toward her bed. "Check her to be sure."

He did. Soberly.

Obviously, I was desperate, but he acted like it was a legitimate request. He raised and then lowered the towel. "She's gone."

I lifted her bed and carried her to the yard.

Preston didn't have to come to my house—he could have sent any one of his men. Remember, that's what I had asked for. After all, Preston has his Exxon to run.

But he knew I needed a lot more than help with my dog. Preston knew I needed someone to care for me.

That was probably the most difficult part of this favor—trying to comfort someone crying. You know what I mean. You want to share something helpful. You hope to be caring, but who knows what to say?

Preston looked down at me. "You're going to be lost without your dog."

That was exactly how I felt.

Only one small sentence, but it comforted me—profoundly. Preston understood, and the fact that he understood was what I needed.

Preston's man, Michael, is young and strong. He dug a very good hole and then looked to his boss for approval.

Preston stepped forward, surveyed the grave, and pointed to one side. "Square it off over there," he said.

Michael nodded. Obviously, this was important. It had to be right.

I clasped the bed tightly with Baby resting there, wanting to place her in the grave myself, but it was deeper than I could reach. Michael took her from me gingerly, as though he was lifting his own newborn. Carefully, he settled Baby into her final resting place.

He lifted the first shovel of dirt, placing it gently at the far end of her bed away from where her head lay beneath the towel.

Fresh tears filled my eyes—it was a great kindness.

Michael is a sensitive person. If he'd thrown dirt in there, I think my heart would have burst open.

I couldn't watch as he lifted the second shovel of dirt into the grave. This part was too final. I retreated to a wall by the edge of my house.

Preston remained as his man finished closing the grave, carefully overseeing the final segment of the job. I tried to pay him, but Preston wouldn't take anything for her burial.

Jay Thomas, my first editor, told me how Preston had helped him, towing his vehicle. "He didn't charge me anything either," Jay said.

Preston has "Jesus Saves" on the side of his Exxon trucks. It's been a year now since Baby died, and I recently learned the story behind that message. He bought his first truck from a man who had "Jesus Saves" painted on it.

A man came by and offered to paint over it. "Let me put the name of your business there," the man said.

"That is my business," Preston answered, knowing everything comes from God.

Jesus said: "You are the light of the world. A city on a hill cannot be hidden . . . In the same way, let your good deeds shine out for all to see, so that everyone will praise your heavenly Father."[1]

When I think of those words, I think of Preston Boutwell. His deeds shine brightly.

May God be praised.

---

1. Matthew 5:14,16 NIV, NLT

Notes, Revelation, Prayers Date:_____
If God moved in your heart, record your notes, revelation, prayers.

PART III

MOST IMPORTANT

21

THE LAMB

NOTHING IS MORE IMPORTANT THAN THIS

"For God so loved the world, that He gave His only begotten Son, that whoever believes in Him shall not perish, but have eternal life."

JOHN 3:16[1]

---

1. NASB

NOTHING IS MORE IMPORTANT
THAN THIS

Six-year-old Sammy knew he was born for basketball. After school, his ball was always with him. Sammy brought it to meals, bobbed it in his bath, and slept with it by his pillow. He'd even taught his parrot to speak his favorite word: basketball!

With the tenacity of a mailman, Sam played in rain, snow, sleet, and gloom of night. After school, nothing came between him and his ball. Except that one day.

Thunder roared over Sammy's head as he shot hoops. Then lightning crackled and split the dark sky.

"Inside, Sammy!" his mom called.

The boy wandered from the living room to the dining room, ball on his hip. He sat at the kitchen window, rolling the ball on his knee. He stared at the sky, lightning still slicing the dark clouds. Before long, he began bouncing his ball.

"Sammy!" his mom called from somewhere in the house. "Dad told you no ball inside!"

The boy eyed the enclosed breezeway—he couldn't be heard out there. "Okay!" he shouted.

And off he went, practicing his dribble, driving the ball between his legs, slamming it from hand to hand. It wasn't hurting anything.

Until it did.

The ball got away from him, hit the wall, and a picture came crashing down. The glass shattered and shards went everywhere.

That evening, his dad eyed him, and Sam saw the disappointment there.

The next day little Sammy knew what he had to do. "Can you fix it?" he asked in earnest, handing the frame across the counter at the hardware store. He hugged his piggybank under one arm.

The old clerk nodded, and Sam shoved all his treasure across the counter.

That night, Sam met his dad at the door with picture in hand. "I'm sorry."

His dad gazed at him gently, scooping him into a hug, and then Sam started crying.

His dad leaned back. "Why so sad, son?"

Sam shook his head, choking on his tears. It was happiness—he and his dad were one again.

Maybe you remember disappointing your parent or grandparent. I remember those times vividly, the shame I felt. I couldn't wait to make it right.

Sammy eyed his dad who sat on his bed that night. "It's time you learned, Sam."

The boy climbed from under the covers and onto his dad's lap. "I paid for it."

"That's not how it works with God."

Sam slid his hand into his dad's. "How does it work?"

"Do you remember learning in Sunday school how God's people were in slavery in Egypt? How God parted the sea so they could flee?"

Sam nodded.

"But then they did terrible things. So God wrote a rulebook. It says what to do when the rules are broken. Disobeying Mom and me is in that rulebook."

The boy tightened his hand in his dad's.

"Sam, the only way a wrong can be wiped away between you and God is with a blood sacrifice."

Sammy straightened.

"God said to take an animal and kill it—a lamb, maybe a bird."

"It died?"

"It had to die. That was the price. Blood had to be shed. God's people needed to see how serious this was—they caused the animal to lose its life."

Sammy glanced toward his bird, big tears filling his eyes.

"God doesn't want Tweety's blood," his dad said. "Not anymore."

His dad lifted him and they knelt by the bed, but Sam didn't understand the words his father prayed.

Years passed and his dad often knelt with him at night, praying the same words. Sammy listened closely, but they never made sense to him.

"We ask forgiveness," his dad would say, "claiming Your sacrifice. Cover my son's wrongs that he might be restored to You."

One night, when Sam was twelve, he suddenly interrupted. "You're claiming the blood of Jesus. You're asking for Jesus' blood to cover my sins so I can be one again with God. Jesus was the sacrifice. Like the animal that was killed!"

"He's the Lamb of God, Sammy." The boy understood it all now.

His dad went on. "Atonement is a great big word that just means 'at-one-ment.' You can break it apart and understand it easily, Sam. Jesus' crucifixion makes us at one with God, if we believe."

Sammy's story is all-important. His dad loves him—nothing the boy can do will ever change that. Nevertheless, when Sam disobeys his father, it separates them.

God loves us the same way, without condition. But disobedience separates us from our Father as surely as it separates Sam from his.

Ask for forgiveness, but that alone won't restore you to God—it's the blood of Christ that removes the wrong.

The Bible says, "If we confess our sins, he is faithful and just to forgive us our sins and to cleanse us . . . the blood of Jesus . . . cleanses us from all sin."[1]

---

1. 1 John 1:9,7 - ESV

That is the power of the Crucifixion—Jesus' blood is the at-one-ment, restoring us to God.

"If we confess our sins, he is faithful and just to forgive us our sins and to cleanse us . . . the blood of Jesus . . . cleanses us from all sin."

Nothing in life is more important than this.

Notes, Revelation, Prayers Date:_____

If God moved in your heart, record your notes, revelation, prayers.

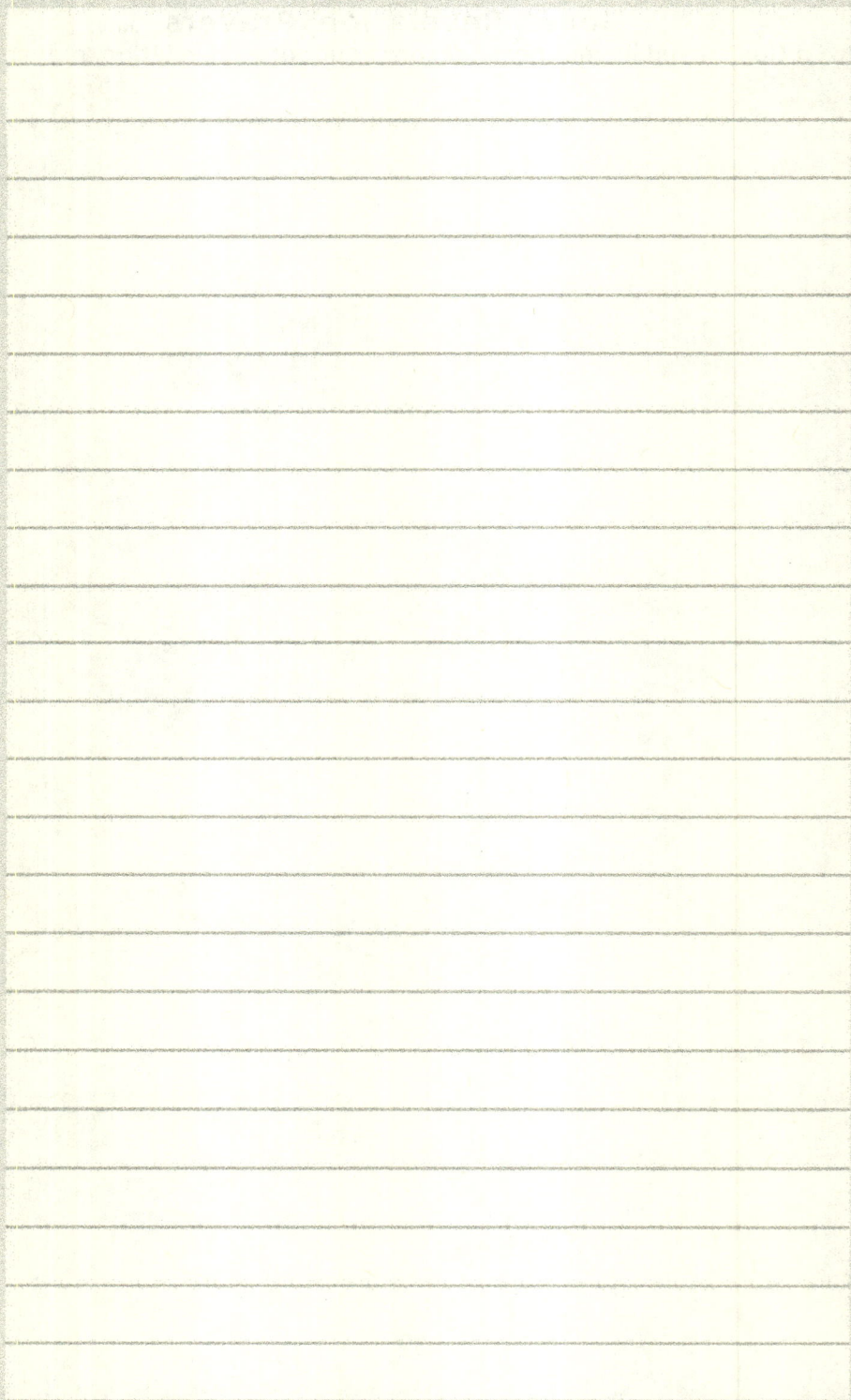

22

THE CENTURION

A SOLDIER'S FAMOUS WORDS OF FAITH

"Share in suffering as a good soldier of Christ Jesus."

2 TIMOTHY 2:3[1]

---

1. ESV

THE SOLDIER'S FAMOUS WORDS OF FAITH

He was not a young soldier. Not a private, first class. He'd risen through the ranks, the equivalent of perhaps a captain or major today.

Scripture identifies him only as "the centurion," obviously a strong, brave man, and apparently in charge of Christ's crucifixion. He was both a disciplined soldier and one capable of great cruelty. The Roman army demanded such abilities.

When he awoke that Friday morning, the centurion could not have known what the day would bring. Romans were heathens, worshipping gods and goddesses, but this soldier would soon speak one of the most famous statements of faith ever recorded in history.

Remember, Jesus is tried in the early morning hours by the Jews. He's then taken to Pilate, who sends Him to Herod. Jesus is sent back to Pilate, condemned, and turned over to soldiers for execution.

The soldiers gather the whole Roman cohort, a battalion of men—perhaps 400. Two Gospels describe almost word for word what happens next. It's remarkable. Apparently, those writers had a source among the soldiers—maybe the man who came to Christ that day.

Jesus is dressed in a fine robe. The soldiers twist together a crown of thorns, placing it on His head. They take a reed, putting it in His right hand. The soldiers kneel and bow before Him, shouting, "Hail King of the Jews!" They spit on Him, beating His head and face with that reed.[1]

Jesus is also scourged; He's beaten. The Roman whip had pieces of metal knotted into it, so as to tear open a man's flesh.

Jesus is then taken to Golgotha where soldiers nail Him to the cross.

The religious leaders had won, yet they arrive at the execution, jeering at the Lord, unable to let it go. Those passing by also hurl abuse at Jesus. Even the soldiers make fun of the Lord: "If you are the King of the Jews, save yourself!"

Jesus responds, "Father, forgive them . . ."

When the Lord speaks these words, was it just for the Jews? Or did Jesus look also at the Roman soldiers? At the centurion? Did Jesus move this hardened soldier?

Scripture states the centurion came and stood at the foot of the cross, right in front of the Lord. A soldier of rank, there's little doubt he'd driven his sword through many men—from the coward fleeing battle to the opponent within arm's reach, that enemy taking a final breath to curse the centurion to his face. This commander wasn't prepared for a completely different Man. For Jesus.

The Lord shouts, "It is finished. Father into Your Hands I commit My Spirit." [2]

And Jesus breathes His last.

Scripture says the centurion begins praising God.[3] And, at this moment, he speaks his famous statement of faith. I'll let the Bible tell you his words.

"When the centurion, who was standing right in front of [Jesus], saw the way He breathed His last, he said, 'Truly this man was the Son of God!'"[4]

1. Matthew 27:27-30, Mark 15:16-19
2. John 19:30, Luke 23:46 - NASB
3. Luke 23:47, NASB
4. Mark 15:39, NASB

The centurion had watched Jesus as He sought forgiveness for those who had bitterly abused Him, and it changed the man.

The ability to truly forgive is a great divider of men and women. Ministers will tell you it's a troubling problem within their congregations.

The matter can cut even deeper.

I am reminded of a small church I attended years ago. Our new minister—the most gifted speaker I'd ever heard—seemed destined to become a world-renowned evangelist. When he preached, you could hear a pin drop.

Yet something seemed amiss. He was nearly forty and hadn't been assigned a larger church.

Soon enough, those beautifully delivered sermons became a problem, and church attendance dwindled.

One Sunday, a deacon approached me, frowning. "The things he says."

"Have you talked to him?" I asked.

He nodded and scowled, even more upset.

I eyed him. "What happens now?"

"We're stuck with him."

So what was the minister's problem? Here's an example. During Bible study, the minister mentioned a man who'd wronged him.

"That jerk!" he said.

See what I mean—the minister hadn't learned to forgive.

As I said, he's not alone. We live in a world that teaches fairness, and forgiveness is the epitome of unfairness—the wrongdoer doesn't deserve to be forgiven.

Every day, remember the crushing death of our Lord. Know that you are His witness to the world. Remember also the centurion standing before the cross, how forgiveness changed his life.

The greater the ordeal, the greater the impact of forgiveness on another.

Hold dear this Bible verse. Memorize it and keep it close: "Share in suffering as a good soldier of Christ Jesus."[5]

Do as Jesus did. Forgive.

---

5.   2 Timothy 2:3, ESV

Notes, Revelation, Prayers Date:_____
If God moved in your heart, record your notes, revelation, prayers.

23

THE MESSIAH
THE FINAL WORDS OF CHRIST

"My God, my God, why have You forsaken me?"

PSALM 22:1[1]

_____

1. NASB

THE FINAL WORDS OF CHRIST

The dying thoughts of any man are significant, but much more so when they belong to Christ.

Jesus made seven statements on the cross, and one has become the subject of many Easter sermons: "My God, my God, why have You forsaken me?"

Preachers often explain by saying Jesus took upon Himself all the sins of the world, and God had to turn away. Ask these same ministers if God is almighty and they will say, "Absolutely!"

Omnipotence means God doesn't *have* to do anything. No amount of sin would be too much for Him. So why say it? Why have many Christians come to accept this limitation on God?

Because we hold Scripture dear, and Jesus said these words—so they must be understood.

I have heard others explain by saying, "Jesus just wanted it over."

Indeed, but that's not the same as claiming Jesus thought God had forsaken Him.

My Lutheran friend explained how her church teaches it. "God definitely didn't leave Jesus," she said. "But our Lord was overwhelmed and *thought* God had left Him."

I growled inside when I heard that any church would teach such a thing. It's completely at odds with the facts.

Was Jesus overwhelmed when stakes were driven into his hands and feet? If our Lord had thought God had deserted Him, this would have been the time.

Instead, look at what Jesus does.

He thinks of his mother's future. Jesus says to her, ". . . behold, your son!," indicating his beloved disciple. And then Jesus says to the disciple, "Behold, your mother!" [1]

Our Lord comforts the thief saying, ". . . today, you will be with Me in Paradise."[2]

Jesus even thinks of those jeering at Him. "Father," He says, "forgive them, for they know not what they do."[3]

And it is Jesus who gives up His own spirit. "Father, into your hands I commit my spirit!"[4] Then Jesus breathes His last.

Our Lord is in control every moment He hangs on the cross.

So if God did not abandon Christ, and if Jesus never felt abandoned, why did our Lord say the words "My God, my God, why have You forsaken me?"[5]

The Jews who stood at the foot of the cross would have known exactly!

Their hope for the Messiah was much greater than ours, as was their understanding of the Old Testament. Moreover, in Jesus' day, the Psalms were not neatly numbered because of the competing influence of the Greek versions of the Bible.

So, when a teacher referred to a Psalm, he couldn't say "Psalm 23." Instead, he would speak the first line.

The first line of Psalm 22 reads: "My God, my God, why have You forsaken me?"

Saying those words was the equivalent of saying "Psalm 22." Jesus

---

1. John 19:26, 27 - ESV
2. Luke 23:43 - ESV
3. Luke 23:34 - ESV
4. Luke 23:46 - ESV
5. Mark 15:34 - ESV

had merely identified a Psalm to his listeners. Not anything more. Nothing ominous!

The Bible confirms this. The word Jesus uses for God proves He was quoting Scripture. Listen to me. Without delving into Greek, Hebrew, and Aramaic, suffice it to say Jesus spoke to God, saying, "Father" or "Dad." It was close and personal.

If Jesus had been addressing God in this statement about being forsaken, why would Jesus suddenly switch to a formal, Old Testament word for God? The word Jesus uses is the exact same word used in Psalm 22.

That's not a coincidence.

There is no doubt Jesus was quoting Psalm 22 and not speaking to God.

Additionally, John, who was at the Crucifixion, leaves Jesus' statement out of his Gospel entirely. Why would John do that?

John wrote his text last and must have seen that non-Jews were having trouble understanding these last words of Jesus, just as many stumble with them today. Instead of repeating Jesus' statement quoting the first line of Psalm 22, John quotes another section of Psalm 22, showing that Jesus fulfills that Scripture:

"So the [guards] said to one another, 'Let us not tear [the tunic], but cast lots for it to decide whose it shall be'; this was to fulfill the Scripture 'They divided My outer garments among them, and for My clothing they cast lots.'"[6]

In other words, John points the reader to the 22nd Psalm, doing exactly what Jesus had done, but in a different way!

And why was Psalm 22 so important to our Lord, considering everything He might have chosen from Scripture as He was dying on the cross?

Because it said everything.

For a thousand years, God's people had sung Psalm 22 knowing it promised the Messiah. Now, the Jews at the Crucifixion could see the Psalm unfolding before them.

---

6. John 19:24 - NASB, quoting Psalm 22:18

The Roman soldiers had nailed Jesus' hands and feet to the cross.

The Psalm says: ". . . they have pierced my hands and feet." Psalm 22:16

Jesus' bones would have been out of joint from hanging from nails.

The Psalm says: "I can count all my bones—" Psalm 22:17

The Romans had gambled for Jesus' clothes.

The Psalm says: ". . . for my clothing they cast lots." Psalm 22:18

But Psalm 22 does more than promise the Messiah. It claims the Lord will be told to coming generations, to a people yet unborn—that all the ends of the earth would turn to the Lord. The Psalm ends triumphantly, and the Jews would have known that.

Today, there are more Christians in the world than adherents to any other faith.

When Jesus said. "Psalm 22," He thereby said, "I am the promised Messiah and this is God's victory!"

Jesus could not have said more, nor said it better.[7]

---

7. Psalm 22 Scripture quotations were taken from the ESV translation of the Holy Bible.

Notes, Revelation, Prayers Date:_____

If God moved in your heart, record your notes, revelation, prayers.

24

SIMON PETER

BREAKFAST ON THE BEACH WITH THE RISEN LORD

"If we confess our sins, He is faithful and just and will forgive us . . ."

I JOHN 1:9[1]

_____

1. NIV

BREAKFAST ON THE BEACH WITH
THE RISEN LORD

At six years old, Billy could count change. He could also be a handful.

"Ninety cents!" He giggled, counting the dimes as his mother drove away from the little country store. He'd brought a dollar for candy and should have had only pennies left. "Miss Ruby is blind as a bat!"

His mother abruptly made a U-turn, parked, and marched him inside.

"But I didn't do anything!" he said.

She eyed him harshly. "Tell Miss Ruby you took her money."

The old woman toddled slowly from the rear of the store. "What's this?"

At 96, she had worked there since the years following the Great Depression.

"I took it." Billy opened his hand with the change. "You gave me dimes instead of pennies."

The woman examined the money closely, adjusting her glasses.

"Billy," his mom said. "Apologize for the rest."

He swallowed hard as they waited, tears rising in his eyes. "I said . . . something . . ."

His mother nudged him.

"Blind as a bat," he blurted out and then buried his head in the old woman's skirts, sobbing. "I'm sorry. I take it back!"

She stepped forward, lowered her worn hand, gently lifted his face, and wiped the tears with her apron. "Reckon I've said worse. You're sorry, so that's that."

Several decades later, Billy gave a speech to his thriving company, sharing what had happened. "That experience," he said, "broke me open. It changed my life."

Not long after Jesus' resurrection, such shame would break open another heart.

It was daybreak and our risen Lord stood alone on the beach of a large lake, waiting. He had built a charcoal fire, grilling bread and fish. There was important business to finish.

A boat appeared offshore.

Jesus knew the seven fishermen onboard, knew they'd been up all night without a catch. He called out, telling them to move the net, and it quickly filled with fish.

"Come and have breakfast," Jesus said to them.

The Lord took bread and fish from the fire and fed them. After breakfast, he eyed Peter.

"Do you love Me...?" Jesus asked.

"Yes, Lord," Peter answered. "You know that I love You."

Jesus asked again, and Peter must have looked deeply at Jesus.

"Yes, Lord," Peter said.

But it was the third time that hurt—Jesus had just placed Simon Peter's shame into that disciple's hands. Peter had denied Jesus three times in the courtyard and, as far as we know, had never confessed his regret.

Jesus had to break Peter, one way or another.

"Do you love me?" Jesus asked a third time.

Peter got the message. Oh, yes. Scripture tells us plainly. "Peter was grieved because [Jesus] said to him the third time, 'Do you love me?'"[1]

---

1. John 21:17, NASB

Many think Peter denied Jesus because of fear. But Jesus knew what was going on with Peter. His flaw. It wasn't fear.

Remember Malchus, the high priest's man. He led those with weapons to the garden to seize Jesus. Peter drew his sword and sliced off Malchus' right ear.[2]

Peter would have fought and died for the Lord. But that wasn't what Jesus wanted. The Lord surrendered, telling his captors to let the disciples go.

And the disciples left, except for Peter, who followed and fearlessly found a way into the courtyard where Jesus had been taken.

Peter needed to stay close to the Lord. That much is clear. And all of what Peter did required great courage. Isn't it possible that Simon Peter denied Jesus to avoid detection, to stay close to Him?

It was only when the cock crowed the third time that Peter realized his mistake. It was then that Jesus turned and looked at him.[3]

Peter still could have said, "I'm with this Man!" Instead, Simon Peter went out and wept.

Peter would have died in the garden fighting for Jesus. Peter wasn't fearful by nature, but he had a flaw. Simon Peter couldn't surrender. He had too much pride. To him, surrender was weakness.

So, there on that beach, Jesus had to deal with Peter's flaw. Jesus is not addressing fear. The Lord needs to break Peter's pride. To show him that surrender is not weakness.

Jesus asked, "Do you love me, Peter?"

Can you follow me this time? Will you surrender yourself for me?

Do you see the difference? Pride can be far worse than fear.

Recently, a woman came and apologized to me. She knew I'd over-heard something she'd said. As she spoke her regret, I could see how much it hurt her.

When you apologize for your misdeeds, when you come forward and say, "I'm sorry," it will break you open.

Billy said, "I never wanted to go through it again."

---

2. John 18:10
3. Luke 22:61

It's for that very reason—because the apology changes us—that God says, "Confess your sins."[4]

Confession has broken me many times. It should hurt. If you can easily tell God your misdeeds, I ask whether you truly love Jesus. You should see your wrongs and say, "Jesus died for this?"

Apologize to those you hurt—it will help them.

It will help you more.

And, always, say you're sorry to God.

---

4. 1 John 1:9

Notes, Revelation, Prayers Date:_____

If God moved in your heart, record your notes, revelation, prayers.

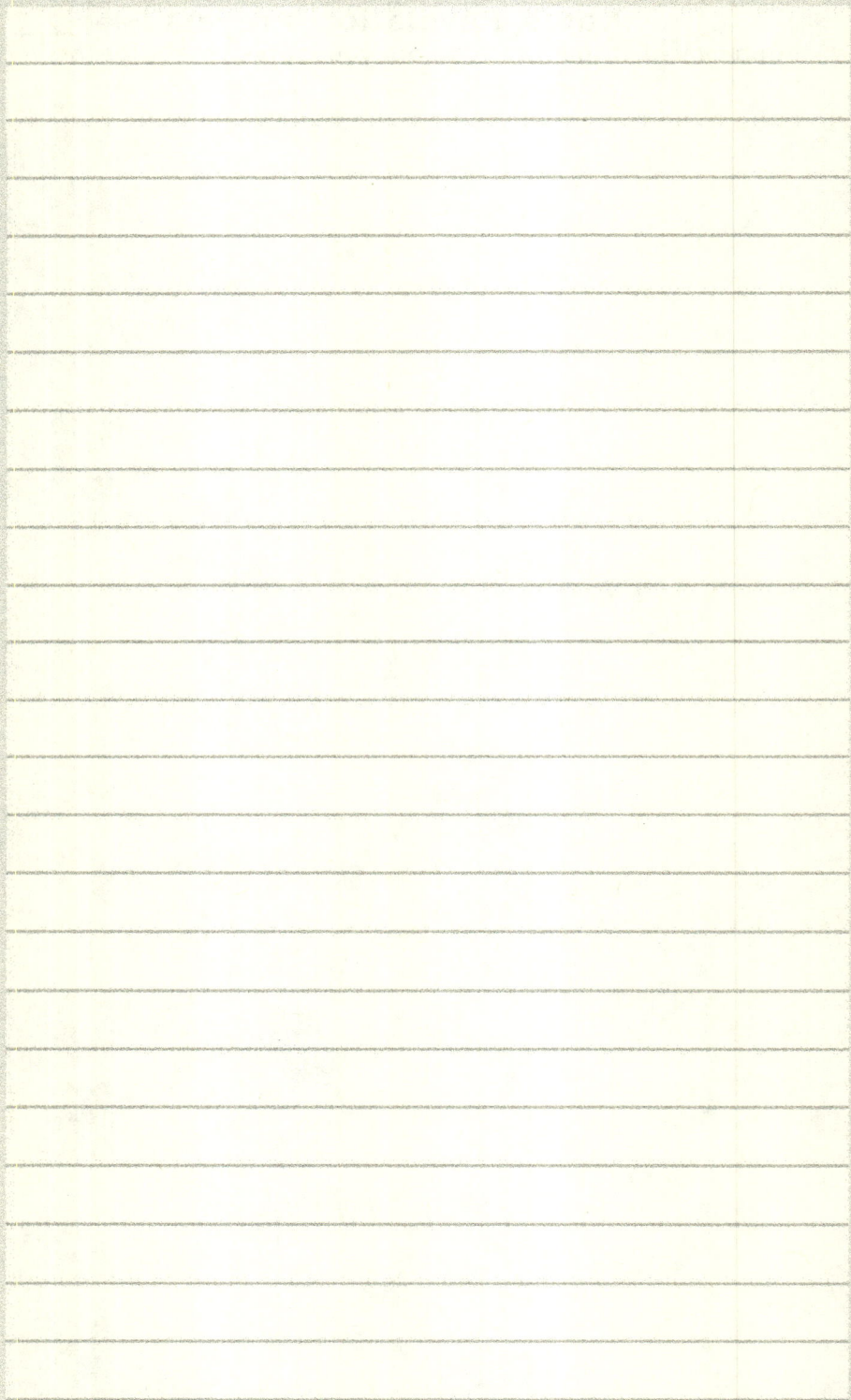

PART IV

THE VALUE OF A STORY

25

JESUS LOVED TO TELL STORIES

PERSEVERANCE

"All Jesus did that day was tell stories—a long storytelling afternoon. His storytelling fulfilled the prophecy: I will open my mouth and tell stories; I will bring out into the open things hidden since the world's first day."

Matthew 13:34-35[1]

---

1. The Message Bible

PERSEVERANCE

Many disdain fiction. Rightfully so. A lot of stories and novels promote evil, one way or another.

Every writer has an agenda—something he or she is trying to convey. I am no different.

I've been a newspaper faith columnist for about a decade, reaching millions with God's word. And I love it!

But two decades before that, I started writing stories. God led me to become a storyteller even earlier, when I was quite young.

All my writing awards are for fiction.

And all of those stories tell God's truths.

Jesus Loved to Tell Stories

Jesus never wrote a book, but He loved to tell stories.

Think of the "Sower and the Seed," the "Prodigal Son," the "Good Samaritan." But that's scarcely a start — consider the "Wandering Sheep," the "Workers in the Vineyard," the "Unmerciful Servant," the "Wedding Banquet," the "Ten Virgins," the "Returning Owner," and on and on it goes.

The Lord's Story on Perseverance

Jesus said, "Suppose one of you has a friend, and goes to him at midnight and says to him, 'Friend, lend me three loaves, because a friend of mine has come to me from a journey and I have nothing to serve him'; and from inside he answers and says, 'Do not bother me; the door has already been shut and my children and I are in bed; I cannot get up and give you anything.'"[1]

I suspect Jesus smiled.

This is how He continued: "I tell you, even if he will not get up and give him anything just because he is his friend, yet because of his shamelessness he will get up and give him as much as he needs." [2]

Why do I think the Lord smiled?

Because the neighbor came, shamelessly beating down the man's door. Not at noon. It was midnight, and Jesus wanted His disciples to understand the value of perseverance.

"So I say to you," Jesus continued, "ask, and it will be given to you; seek, and you will find; knock, and it will be opened to you . . . which one of you fathers will his son ask for a fish, and instead of a fish, he will give him a snake? . . . So if you . . . know how to give good gifts to your children, how much more will your heavenly Father give the Holy Spirit to those who ask Him?"[3]

Thus, Jesus told His disciples, God cares for you. But He also taught them to persevere."

Christian rocker Toby Mac echoed Jesus' message with his hit "Move." He sings: "I know your heart been broke again. I know your prayers ain't been answered yet. I know you're feeling like you got nothing left. Well, lift your head, it ain't over yet . . . Keep walkin', soldier keep movin' on . . . "

See how Toby Mac creates a story with music? The soldier lifts his head and perseveres, knowing God cares for him.

---

1. Luke 11:5-7
2. Luke 11:8
3. Luke 5:9-13

Keep walking. Keep moving on.

Whatever has discouraged you, whatever you need from the Lord, keep praying.

Persevere.

Do not give up.

God is with you and He cares for you.

Notes, Revelation, Prayers Date:_____

If God moved in your heart, record your notes, revelation, prayers.

EXCERPT

EMERALD COAST: THE VENDETTA

"So do not fear, for I am with you; do not be dismayed, for I am your God. I will strengthen you and help you; I will uphold you with my righteous right hand."

Isaiah 41:10[1]

---

1. NIV

THE STORY

I n this final chapter, I included the Prologue to "Emerald Coast," a series that will leave you with a great truth about your walk with the Lord.

Emerald Coast: The Vendetta is Volume 1 of the series.

This *Law and Order* type story with political overtones follows young investigator Jase McLain, who lands a job babysitting a mogul's beach house on the Emerald Coast of Florida. All goes well until his famous neighbor is nearly assassinated.

First on the scene, Jase saves the celebrity, who tells him a three-word clue before slipping into a coma. That clue will lead Jase not only to the shooter but also through a web of political intrigue.

Emerald Coast is a multi-volume, sweeping story that shows one man's faith. I will add the disclaimer that there is no foul language in *Emerald Coast*, but it does have violent scenes.

If suspense is not your thing, I have a funny romantic mystery coming in 2025.

Jesus knew a well-crafted tale could stay with you for a lifetime. He never wrote a book, but Jesus loved to tell stories.

"Jesus said to them, 'Therefore every scribe who has become a disciple of the kingdom of heaven is like a head of a household, who brings out of his treasure new things and old.'"

Matthew 13: 52[1]

_____

1. NASB

PROLOGUE

EMERALD COAST: THE VENDETTA

Thursday afternoon
September 30

They were in uniform—state troopers, county deputies, municipal police. Mostly men. Their wives walked beside them quietly in black dresses and low heels. Each carried a covered glass dish of food.

The two-lane country road lined with parked law enforcement vehicles had a narrow space down the middle for anyone who needed to travel that road.

It went on for a quarter mile and there were still more vehicles coming. Since there wasn't nearly enough room for them, several law enforcement officers had taken charge, directing vehicles into the acreage that surrounded the prim white house, creating a wide, well-organized parking lot.

The late afternoon light faded to darkness as over a thousand mourners stood in groups outside the house, either beside cars, in the yard, or across the wide porch that circled the rear part of the house.

The wives moved among the mourners, refilling glasses as everyone ate from paper plates piled high with food. Each person expressed condolences to Moses, many recounting loving memories of his wife. Moses ran law enforcement, one way or another, for the whole Florida Panhandle and was the most respected lawman on the East Coast.

They all knew his son had made the prestigious Central Investigations Division on Monday. At thirty, Jase was now the youngest investigator on the force. But there had been no celebration—his mother had died that same day.

Jase heard a crying child in the crowd and a dad unable to soothe her. "Jase!" the four-year-old shouted, running to him. "Blue-Boo is gone!"

"Not Blue-Boo!" Jase gave her his full attention.

The child nodded, now bravely trying not to cry as Jase lowered his six-foot-four frame and faced her. He glanced up and nodded to the man with her, the Pensacola police chief.

"I'm sorry, Jase." The man winced as he spoke. "Our sitter got sick, and she promised to be good." He looked at his daughter. "Let's not bother Jase with this today. I'll come back and look for Blue-Boo tomorrow, honey."

"Nooo!" the little girl wailed and began to cry fiercely.

"That's not necessary, Chief," Jase said. He pointed the girl across the yard to the big hand of a clock above the porch. "Watch the longer one going around. When it reaches the top, I'll send out a posse. Before it reaches the top again, we'll have Blue-Boo."

"Really?" The little girl exploded with hope. "Do you promise?"

"I do." Jase tapped her nose. "You're in the right place, Peyton. We have a fairly experienced group here."

She wrapped an arm around his neck as he lifted her and crossed the yard. They eyed the clock and waited for the big hand to hit twelve.

"Listen up!" Jase said, climbing the steps to the porch, turning in a circle, surveying those around him and then the massive crowd in the yard. "I have an APB. Anyone see a blue bunny?"

"He's fuzzy," the child whispered as she shyly buried her head in his chest. "Tell them his name is Blue-Boo."

"Said bunny answers to Blue-Boo," Jase told the crowd. "And he's fuzzy. Not to be confused with the regular blue bunnies."

A hand shot up from the group, waving the long floppy ears of a chubby stuffed rabbit. "Blue-Boo in custody, sir!"

A roar of laughter, clapping, and cheers went up.

All watched as the bunny sailed through the air, bouncing overhead from one officer's outstretched hand to another until it reached Jase. As the little girl hugged it, she pointed to the clock. "Look, Jase!" The big hand had just reached the twelve. "You were right!"

He gave the child to her grateful father and turned to see a young woman with substantial curves smiling up at him. "Ye are a good man, Jase McLain," she said with an Irish lilt, butting her shoulder into his side. "Yes, ye are."

He brushed back her red hair and kissed her on the forehead. "A ceadsearc."

"Stop it!" she whispered, looking around.

Moses stepped to them and clapped Jase around the shoulder. "Well done, son."

Seconds ticked by as a gentle, quiet spell wrapped itself around the three, time standing still. It was a rare moment of joy in five awful months.

Maureen spoke first, glancing at her watch. "It's almost nine. I have to go. They let me switch to midnights for tonight."

Both men watched as she gathered her things. She blew them a kiss, which both of the broad-shouldered giants returned. Maureen then hurried away.

Hours passed and the evening grew late. Slowly, one by one, the mourners trailed back down the road and into the makeshift parking areas—the women carrying their now-empty dishes.

By midnight, they had all climbed into their vehicles and were gone.

———

JASE LISTENED to the suddenly quiet house as he made his way down the center hallway. He stopped midway and stared into his mother's room.

Moses had placed a rope there days ago, silently informing any visitor to keep out.

Jase eyed the polished wood floor. He thought of the first time he'd looked inside, staring with wonder at the wall of mirrors.

He stood there a moment and then stepped over the rope. Jase sat down, eyeing the ballet barre that stretched the length of the room. He could still see her watching him all those years ago.

"Come, Jase," she had said.

"I, I no—" His English wasn't good.

"Dance with me." The smile in her voice delighted him—this young woman suddenly in his life.

Jase remembered climbing to his feet slowly, staring at his tiny new tennis shoes. He was barely five.

"I, I no dance, Ms. Myrrh."

"It's Mama." She reached for his hand and showed him how to move his feet. He tripped again and again, but she patiently stepped with him. "Ladies love a man with moves, Jase."

"The boy doesn't care." A voice, deep and graveled, came from the hall. Moses stood there, all six-foot-four inches of him, carved from stone. He leaned against the door frame.

"Boys grow into men." She eyed him with a wicked grin.

Jase remembered the two and smiled to himself. He hadn't understood at the time.

Moses strutted his massive frame into the room and took her into his arms. "Let me show you, son."

Jase quickly retreated to his spot on the floor, watching with stunned delight as their bodies moved together quickly. He'd never seen anything like it.

———

SIX LARGE BLACK SUVs quietly navigated the streets of New York City.

The vehicles moved forward until they reached a private airport and a plane waiting there.

It was after midnight and the bright lights of the city could be seen in the distance. None of the passengers had a hint as to where the aircraft was headed. It was a stealth mission.

They only knew that the plane would return within hours, carrying priceless, one-of-a-kind treasure.

———

JASE SAT on that polished wood floor opposite the mirrors, thinking of the couple in their mid-twenties who couldn't have children and how they had taken him in.

Abruptly, he turned his head. Jase could hear glass breaking and the memory vanished, replaced by two men arguing in a distant room.

Jase heard a crash and then a blistering explosion—the Italian had thrown the bottle of gin into the fireplace. It wasn't the first time.

Doesn't matter, Jase thought. *Everyone has gone.*

Jase rested his head back against the wall as the two men kept shouting. The argument grew louder as the two moved down the hall.

"You're accepting it, Moses!" the Italian yelled.

"I dohhn't want it!" The words slurred.

"You'll be the top dog in the state."

"Not tahhking it!"

"Moses, you've done everything they wanted. The tests. The drills. And you got it!"

Jase nodded. *You did it, Moses!*

Jase could not have been more proud of the man who'd reared him.

The letter had come to the house while they were at the graveside —Moses had been chosen to head DOCS, the brand-new Department of Capitol Security at the statehouse in Tallahassee. He was about to be the highest paid and most important law enforcement officer in the state of Florida.

"I'm nohht tahhking it!" Moses staggered past the door.

"Yes, you are!" the Italian shouted.

"I dohhn't have to. Not anymore."

Jase listened closely.

Moses' voice trailed off. "I'm free—I'm finally free—"

Jase jumped to his feet. He charged out of the room and down the hall toward the two men as Moses disappeared into his bedroom. The Italian quickly blocked Jase's path.

"He didn't mean it, boy," the Italian said.

"Let me pass."

"He's drunk. He'll sleep it off—"

"Let me pass!" Jase tried to get around Carlo Rigatonni, who was short and no match for Jase's size and strength, which equaled Moses'. But the Italian had trained Jase when he'd first come on the force, and Jase respected him.

"Let me pass, Carl!"

"And do what?"

Jase kept trying to get around the small man.

"Let it go, boy. You need to get down to the beach."

Jase could feel the tears on his face and wiped them back furiously. "He loved her!"

"Of course he did," the Italian said. "Now go!"

———

THE PRIVATE PLANE flew in darkness, following the coastline of the Florida Panhandle. Daybreak was hours away, and the aircraft's shining lights looked conspicuous, even urgent, as it began to descend.

The moon silently cast long rays of light over the black waters of the Gulf, and the lone man swimming in its sheen stopped to watch the aircraft.

There were three military bases within a fifty-mile radius, so Jase was used to seeing military aircraft at any hour. Except this was not a military plane. And it was descending and about to land nearby.

———

MOSES STOOD naked at the end of his couch, staring down at the man sleeping there. "What are you doing here, Carl?"

The Italian opened his eyes and sat up quickly, rubbing his face. "You need to call the boy."

"Why?"

Carl Rigatonni reached for his hat and stood. "Just do it, Moses."

"Why?"

Carl cleared his throat and began to explain. Before he finished, Moses pulled on his boots, strutted past him, and slammed out of the house, wearing nothing but his Stetson.

————

SIX MEN LEANED against the fence of the private airport in Monarch, Florida, watching the plane moving along the runway. Behind them, six black SUVs idled quietly, their windows darkened for privacy.

"Any idea who it is?" the youngest driver asked the others.

When no one answered, he took several steps toward the plane. As it came to a halt and the door opened, all six of the drivers straightened. They heard men with thick accents arguing loudly.

————

JASE SWAM hard through the black waters of the Gulf. All he wanted was to stop hearing Moses in his head.

On the beach behind him stood the most elegant house in the area, built by one of the wealthiest men in the nation. Jase had just landed the off-duty assignment of a lifetime, babysitting the house every night.

It stood in a small, gated enclave called Morning Tides Village. Beside the house were three more homes and an empty lot, all lining the beach. Farther back, another handful of homes dotted the small area. That was it—the entire village.

In stark contrast, right up against the little enclave, opulent resorts lined the beach with their high-rise condos that faced the Gulf. That was to the west.

To the east, there was nothing but virgin coastland—a protected preserve would keep the area just as it had been when settlers first stepped onto that shore.

Jase closed his eyes, desperately wishing Moses' words away. And then he heard the man swimming beside him.

The water was shallow, and Jase stood, looking at him.

Moses also stood.

Before Jase could speak, he heard the graveled voice.

"What were you thinking, son?" Moses' anger rippled just below the surface of his voice.

Jase didn't answer him.

"What?" Moses said. "You lived in that house from the time you were five and you don't think I loved her?"

"I know you did." Jase fought the emotion rising in his eyes. "I know that."

"Then what?"

Jase only wanted to put the awful memory out of his mind.

"What?"

"I—" Jase heard his voice tremble and turned away as a tear skidded down his cheek. But Moses circled him. Both men, the same height and weight, stood face to face.

"Heard what?"

Jase couldn't speak. Couldn't breathe.

Moses stepped closer. "Answer me, son."

"You said—" The words tore his heart open.

"What?"

"You were free of her."

"I never said that!" He spoke barely above a whisper, but there was a wild fury in his voice. "Think good and hard."

"I know you loved her, Moses."

"And don't you *ever* forget it."

At that, Moses turned and strutted through the shallow water to the shore. Moments later, he was gone.

———

THE SIX SUVs paraded in a line down Highway 98 for miles, passing one high-rise condo after another. When they finally reached a forested area, the caravan slowed to a halt.

The first SUV turned onto a narrow blacktop road and stopped at the arm of an unmanned gate barring entry. The driver eyed the envelope on the seat beside him. It had been sealed when the pilot handed it to him.

"It's your destination," the pilot had said. "I was instructed to wait here."

The driver had opened it quickly. The card inside read: "Morning Tides Village – pink beach house – No. 116 Amber Drive." Beneath it was a phone number.

As a local, the driver knew where the community sat, tucked quietly away from Highway 98. But there was no code for the gate.

He hurried back to the driver behind him. The two made the call, and then the first driver ran back, entered the code on the panel, and the gate lifted.

One by one, the six vehicles passed through.

The road threaded into dense, dark woods as deer milled about. The first driver moved slowly, letting them cross in front of him and move to grassy spaces that lined the road.

When the driver reached the top of a small mound, he suddenly saw the Gulf of Mexico spreading out before him in the distance. He stopped and smiled, gazing at the unexpected beauty of a path of moonlight reflecting off the black water.

Immediately, the man in the back began yelling in his thick accent.

Not the first time.

The driver eyed his GPS and headed down the hill toward the four homes that lined the beach. He pulled in front of the pink one.

———

BECARDI RUM STUMBLED onto the rear porch of the pink beach house, designer Cernau Fojeau's hand against her back, roughly shoving her forward.

"Do not get the things on the dress, Beecardi!" he shouted in his thick accent. "No things, silly leetle girl!"

She eyed him. *I'm twenty-three. And a lawyer.*

He and his brother had arrived nearly an hour ago with their entourage and had loudly taken command of everyone and everything in sight.

The designer turned back to the house. "I must see about my lovely precious now. No things, Beecardi!"

She heard him barking orders as soon as the screen door slammed behind him, tearing into one assistant after another.

It was too dark to see. All Becardi had in her hand was a penlight and the article that would appear in the afternoon *New York Journal*. The title read, "World's Most Beloved Actress, Victoria Winterhaven, Weds." It would accompany sunrise photos of the star and her bridal party taken by the finest photographer in the world, Fraccai Fojeau.

The interviewer in the article asked Victoria to share a favorite quote.

"For lovely eyes," Victoria said, "seek out the good in people."

"You are often compared with Kate Middleton for your kindness," the interviewer continued. "But what gives you so much confidence?"

"I know Who walks behind me."

Becardi smiled. *That's all true.*

Becardi hated being hot-tempered and wished she could be more like Victoria.

Becardi abruptly lifted her eyes, remembering the photo shoot. The soft morning light would come quickly, and then they would have about thirty minutes before sunrise.

She heard the old man inside the house grumbling. "My daughter is better off dead than married to vermin!"

Becardi turned, watching E. E. Winterhaven as he stepped from the house onto the porch.

"Oh, good," he scoffed. "Look who's out here."

Becardi wanted to be excited about the wedding. She liked Victoria, but her father's marriage to the actress would make billionaire E. E. Winterhaven her grandfather. Neither of them was happy about it.

"Coco!" he yelled. "The numbers!"

Becardi knew the house numbers were proof positive of what *she* was getting from this marriage.

A mean, demented fuddy-duddy.

The old man walked across the porch and picked up the metal numbers, which should have been on the house announcing the address at 116 Amber Drive. But they were always on the floor.

Becardi eyed him. *Because someone can't seem to remember what he keeps saying he's going to do.*

"I'll get them fixed," Becardi said.

"No, you won't!" E. E. Winterhaven shouted.

"I don't mind."

"This is not your house!"

It wasn't his either but she decided against starting a fight over who owned what.

Becardi watched as the striking blonde stepped onto the porch and moved beside him, handing the old man a hammer. She began straightening his tuxedo.

Coco Winterhaven was a good twenty years his junior, which still made her nearly seventy, but she looked amazing.

Becardi smiled. *Thanks to well-spent money.*

Becardi knew the way Coco handled Useless announced that she was his wife and clearly in charge of such womanly matters as his wardrobe.

"Coco, let go of me." He pointed to the house numbers. "I need to nail these down before they fly off and kill Victoria."

He pounded away at the numbers until they were halfway back on the house.

"I'm going to kill her anyway," he mumbled aloud. "How can she do this to you? Shaming her mother—marrying that worthless bum."

"Shhhh." Coco said it to the old man but glanced toward her.

Becardi started down the porch steps, scowling, feeling a tension starting in her shoulders. She told herself to be polite.

Victoria is the lucky one. My dad is wonderful!

"What is it, Coco?" he said. "That thing?"

Becardi knew he was referring to her. She stopped and turned back to him, watching as Coco flashed her an apologetic smile. Becardi thought Coco Winterhaven had all the charm of a Southern debutante, which only made Useless look ridiculously uncouth next to her.

"Why are you shushing me?" he said. "*It* knows it. Her father is a no-good vagrant and gigolo!"

Becardi tightened her lips. *He is not!*

She had promised her dad she wouldn't start anything—and *she* hadn't. "Come along, Useless." Becardi knew it would set him off. And it did.

"Eustice!" he shouted. "A fine family name!" The old man stomped to the edge of the porch. "Your daddy named you after liquor."

"Your daddy named you *Useless*." Becardi knew no one ever talked back to E. E. Winterhaven, and she loved prodding him.

"It's Eustice!" He turned to his wife, clearly at a loss for words. "A fine family name!"

He pounded the hammer on the side of the porch, obviously trying to make a point. "My daughter, Victoria Winterhaven, married to a penniless hobo with a mouthy kid! At least I can give the bum a job, but what can I do with a smart-alecky kid?"

Becardi grinned. "Smart-alecky *grandkid* to you, Bubby."

"Do not call me Bubby. I'm not Jewish!"

"Anti-Semitic?" she said.

"What?"

Becardi laughed. "It means prejudiced, Useless."

He pounded the hammer again. "I *know* what it means. I'm not prejudiced—I'm Presbyterian!"

Becardi lifted her head, listening to the Fojeau brothers yelling inside the house. The *New York Journal* had commissioned them for the clothes and photo shoot. The two hadn't stopped arguing since they had stepped out of the SUVs, which were now idling on the road, ready to hurry them back to their waiting jet.

The Fojeau brothers had flown from New York, bringing the wedding gown and the one bridesmaid's dress. The gowns, the trip, the shoot—all of it had been executed with the utmost secrecy. You couldn't be too careful when it was Victoria Winterhaven. The paparazzi were waiting and watching in their sleep. Each of the photos would become a priceless treasure.

Becardi knew the dresses had been handmade in Italy, or Eastern Europe, or wherever the Fojeaus were from.

She ran a hand down the front of her dress, caressing the expensive fabric. It was silk, woven just for Victoria and her bridesmaid, and then encrusted with precious jewels.

One photography assistant after another dashed past Becardi as she stepped through the sand. They raced back and forth from Victoria's house to the place where the tripods stood. Obviously, it had become the photographer's Mecca, the chosen site, the best location for the shoot.

Each assistant carried all sorts of things, and Becardi studied every piece of equipment they dropped near her. She had no idea what it was all called or what it did.

There were several large reflectors and screens, and one case after another, both large and small, dotting the space around the tripods.

Becardi looked up at the sky. It was getting lighter now.

There isn't a whole lot of time.

She wasn't sure if New Yorkers knew how fast a sunrise happened. And there clearly couldn't be a do-over for these shots. The wedding was that afternoon.

The sun would dance on the horizon for mere moments, and then, without warning, the ball of gold would lift off and be high in the sky. If the photographs weren't taken at that exact moment, just as the sun hit the horizon, they would be lost forever.

"What is that?" Fraccai Fojeau said, coming up behind her.

Becardi eyed the world-famous photographer, who had abruptly stopped arguing with his designer brother. That's because Cernau Fojeau had a new target. He stooped down, grousing at her, fussily brushing sand from the hem of her dress. "I said *no things on the dress*, Beecardi!"

She blinked at him. "It's sand."

The designer stood and met her gaze, glaring. "Leeft. Leeft the creation as you walk. Are you Neanderthull? Leeft it up!"

Becardi saw Fraccai Fojeau still scanning the Gulf. The photographer grabbed binoculars from a bag, peered through them for only a moment, and then ran fully dressed toward the Gulf.

"Yoo-hoo!" he yelled.

Becardi quickly picked up the binoculars. The sky was even lighter, and she could see a figure—a man who had been swimming. But he had stopped and now stood in the water.

Becardi felt as if someone had just punched her in the gut. "So beautiful," she said, barely able to speak, staring at broad shoulders, a sculpted chest, and the rippling of tight ab muscles. Her eyes lingered there as he wiped water from his face and turned toward the horizon. He hadn't noticed anyone on the shore.

Becardi watched as the man lifted an arm burgeoned with heavy muscle and ran a massive hand through his hair. He kept looking toward the horizon, obviously waiting for the sunrise.

His strong back narrowed at the waist and waves of water revealed that he wore nothing but a holster of sorts, riding low on his hips. As he moved, she could see the holster strapped to his thigh with a huge knife inside.

———

JASE STOOD in the waters of the Gulf of Mexico, looking toward the horizon. He didn't know then that his closest neighbor was Victoria Winterhaven, that she would marry in the afternoon, and that by nightfall he would find her shot and nearly dead, whispering three words before slipping into a coma.

Jase would turn the words over a thousand times, netting zero.

UNTIL ONE MONTH LATER . . .

ALSO BY R.A. MATHEWS

I. The Reaching to God Series

Available Now

Vol. 1 Reaching to God, Joy: The Joy of His Presence

Vol. 2 Reaching to God, Hope: The Hope of the Ages

Upcoming Release

Vol. 3 Reaching to God, Christmas: Oh Holy Night

Vol. 4 Reaching to God, Love: His Love Endures Forever

II. The Emerald Coast Series

Available Now

Vol. 1 Emerald Coast: The Vendetta

Upcoming Release

Vol. 2 Emerald Coast: The Fugitive

ABOUT R.A. MATHEWS

Acclaimed theologian Rev. R.A. Mathews graduated from the highest-ranked Baptist seminary in the nation with a Master of Divinity degree and four years of graduate study. She completed extensive Bible research from 2015 to 2024.

Mathews is also an award-winning writer, and her weekly newspaper columns (newspaper articles) about the Lord have been published over 6,000 times across the U.S. and overseas.

This volume contains both inspiring stories from the Bible and misunderstood Scripture—all supported with footnotes leading the reader to the verses in the Bible.

Mathews completed her university education at the age of 21 and started seminary that same year. She then sought ordination and was examined and approved by a panel of pastors and the association of American Baptist Churches to which her church belongs. She is perhaps the first Baptist woman to receive such an ordination in the South.

The Rev. Mathews subsequently worked in Christian broadcasting and in local churches, preaching and working with children and youth.

Like the Apostle Paul, she is bi-vocational, having graduated from a top ten ranked law school with an American Jurisprudence Award in mediation. She mediates disputes and represents children and the mentally challenged.

Mathews is the author of the *Reaching to God* series and a multi-volume serial novel, *Emerald Coast,* written under the pen name Red R.A. Mathews, which draws on her experiences as a state legislator.

She is the granddaughter of the Rev. Cora Hughes, an ordained Nazarene minister.

Visit her at RAMathews.com.

READ FREE & DISCOUNTS

I. YOU CAN READ FREE

You can read a new chapter free every week. Just ask the Editor or Features Editor at your newspaper to contact us, and we'll send your local newspaper a complimentary column every week. Then read free!

Make that call today, send an email, or stop by your newspaper with your book. Talk to your newspaper editor.

Editors are in the business of selling papers and want to hear from you.

II. R.A. MATHEWS BOOK CLUB

Join the R.A. Mathews Book Club and receive discount coupons and more! We also send out free Advance Reader Copies of her books.

We would also like to offer your study group a discount on multiple copies of this book.

Join at RAMathews.com

PASS IT ALONG

If this book has helped you, write about it on Amazon.
It's easy, 3 little steps:

1. Go to Amazon.com
2. Type in "Reaching to God Hope R.A. Mathews"
3. Scroll down and click *Write a Review*.

Your words might help another person:
someone who needs a little bit of encouragement.

TO JOSHUA & TO YOU

When Moses died, Joshua was chosen to lead Israel—to invade and
conquer the Promised Land. This is what God said to him.
It's also what He says to you.

**"Keep this Book of the Law always on your lips; meditate on it day
and night . . . Do not be afraid; do not be discouraged, for the Lord
your God will be with you wherever you go."**

Joshua 1:8-9[1]

---

1. NIV

AFTERWORD

"Sharing Scripture—offering you my love for God—is the greatest joy of a lifetime. Thank you for reading!"

— R.A. MATHEWS

www.ingramcontent.com/pod-product-compliance
Lightning Source LLC
Chambersburg PA
CBHW031829090426
42741CB00005B/177